The Clue in the Ruined Castle

The Famous JUDY BOLTON Mystery Stories

By MARGARET SUTTON

In Order of Publication

A JUDY BOLTON Mystery

The Clue in the Ruined Castle

BY
Margaret Sutton

Illustrated by Pelagie Doane

APPLEWOOD BOOKS
Bedford, Massachusetts

The Clue in the Ruined Castle
was originally published in 1955.

Reprinted by permission of the estate of Margaret Sutton.
All Rights Reserved.

———————

For a complete list of titles in the Judy Bolton Mysteries,
please visit judybolton.awb.com.

Thank you for purchasing an Applewood Book.
Applewood reprints America's lively classics—books from
the past that are still of interest to modern readers.
For a free copy of our current catalog, write to:

Applewood Books
P.O. Box 365
Bedford, MA 01730
www.awb.com

ISBN 978-1-4290-9046-9

MANUFACTURED IN THE U.S.A.

The log was now safely in place

A Judy Bolton Mystery

THE CLUE IN THE
RUINED CASTLE

BY

Margaret Sutton

Grosset & Dunlap

PUBLISHERS   NEW YORK

To Friends and Relatives
from Potter County, Pennsylvania,
site of a real ruined castle

Contents

ix

CHAPTER I

A Lost Castle

"It's ready now, isn't it?" asked Judy when Mrs. Bolton had placed a tempting dish of mixed fruit on the breakfast tray she was preparing. "Shall I take it up to Horace?"

"I wish you would, dear," her mother replied. "I've been up and down those stairs so many times that I'm just about exhausted. Keeping that brother of yours quiet is not so easy as your father seems to think. It's a virus infection of some kind, and Horace simply must stay in bed."

"I'll see that he does," Judy promised. "I've had experience keeping Peter quiet these last few days. He insists he's completely recovered from that terrible experience on the Haunted Road, but I'm not so sure.

He's in Dad's office now, having a check-up. Aren't you glad we stopped in, Mother? I can see you need help."

Judy, married while still in her teens, felt like a little girl again, helping her mother instead of doing her own housework back in Dry Brook Hollow where she and Peter lived. Taking the tray, she tried balancing it on one hand, but gave up at a look from Mrs. Bolton.

"Please, Judy—"

"I know, Mums, act my age."

"I guess you never will," Mrs. Bolton said fondly. "But probably it's just as well. Some people act as if they'd never been children."

"Meaning people like that unpleasant-looking man waiting in Dad's office? He didn't like it when Peter went in ahead of him, but Peter was first."

Judy's mother smiled.

"That sounds like Mr. Boggs. I shouldn't say so, but I was told he became soured on life when he moved into that gloomy old castle—"

"Castle!" exclaimed Judy. "It isn't the castle Dad told us about, is it, Mother? Peter and I are on our way there now. I thought we would explore it just for fun. You know, the way we used to explore places like—well, like the attic of this house, and a hundred other places where we've unearthed mysteries. But if someone lives there, it sort of spoils our plan, doesn't it?"

"I'm afraid it does," Mrs. Bolton agreed, "unless, of course, the people who live there invite you in. They may be friendly. Mr. Boggs is only the caretaker."

"He is?" Judy thought of the expensive car she had seen parked before the house. "They must pay him well. Who owns this—this castle?"

"I don't seem to recall the name. You might ask Horace," Mrs. Bolton suggested.

"I will." Judy hurried on upstairs. In her eagerness to ask her brother about the castle he had once written up for the Farringdon paper, she practically flew. Successfully balancing the tray on one hand, she knocked on the door of her brother's room with the other.

"Food," she announced. "Are you interested?"

"Not much," he answered in a listless voice, "but come in anyway. The medicine Dad gave me has taken away my appetite as well as my fever. Frankly, I feel like a wrung-out dishrag. What brought you here so early in the morning?"

"Fate," said Judy. "Peter is with me. We came in the new car."

Horace moved over so that he could see out the window.

"It's not that futuristic light blue job, is it?" he asked in surprise.

Judy laughed. "Hardly. That belongs to a patient of Dad's. You can't see our car from the window. It's a very inconspicuous black sedan. I named it the Beetle, and for us it's perfect. There are dozens like it. If we want to follow somebody we won't be spotted. Now, your convertible—"

"Unique of its kind," Horace interrupted, "and would I like to be in it! There's a birthday party coming up soon that I want to report."

"Birthday party?" echoed Judy with a giggle. "Do you consider that news?"

"Yes—when there are a hundred candles on the cake."

"A hundred candles!" exclaimed Judy. "I never saw anyone that old, and I think I'd like to. Whose birthday is it?"

Horace ate a little of the food Judy had brought him, before he answered. She suspected he was deliberately keeping her in suspense.

"Would you really like to know?" he finally asked.

"Stop teasing me," Judy scolded. "Of course I would."

"And if I told you it was the birthday of an old lady who grew up in a castle, would you believe it?"

"I might," Judy replied. "I'm ready to believe anything this morning. Mother just told me people lived in the ruined castle you wrote up for the paper, and that's pretty hard to believe. Peter and I are planning to spend the day there."

"Doing what, may I ask?"

"Oh, just exploring and stuff," Judy replied airily. "We've brought along a picnic lunch."

"I don't know where you'll eat it," Horace said. "There's a wall around the castle and 'No Trespassing' signs all over the place. You can't get near it. Actually, that article I wrote was little more than a rehash of the county's history. I never did get inside the castle."

"You didn't?" Judy was surprised to hear this. "I had an idea you'd been all through it."

"Not me," Horace said. "There was an ogre at the door in the form of the caretaker. He wouldn't let anybody in. Said the master didn't wish to be disturbed."

"What about the mistress?" asked Judy.

"You mean the caretaker's wife? I don't know that he has one."

"No, I mean the old lady who is going to celebrate her hundredth birthday. What's she like?"

"I don't know much about her," Horace admitted. "She won't see people. The neighbors say she's suspicious of everybody. She slammed the door in my face—"

"The castle door?"

"No, she doesn't live there any more. But if you can get her to talk, her memories of the castle may make quite a history. I was told by one of her neighbors that she used to go back there to visit. I don't know if she still does." Horace pushed his tray aside. "There's so much I don't know, Sis, and this was my opportunity to find out. The old lady lives with her great-grandson in a farmhouse about a mile below the castle. I believe there are a couple of great-great-grandchildren, but I'm not sure. Could you find out for me, Sis?"

"Could I!" Judy exclaimed. "I can't think of anything I'd rather do. Hurry up and get well, Horace. Maybe they'll celebrate her birthday in the castle and we'll all be invited."

"Maybe, but I wouldn't count on it. She may not be welcome at the castle any more. The neighbors say she started a feud in the family when she married Emil Joerg. She was born Hilma Olsen, and her father was Lars Olsen, a famous violinist with dreams of becoming lord of a Norwegian settlement in Pennsylvania. Sounds strange, doesn't it?"

"It certainly does," agreed Judy.

"Well, the story of how he built the castle and then lost it is stranger still."

"Lost it?" Judy was puzzled. "How could anyone lose a castle?"

"By building it on someone else's land," said Horace. "Legend has it that he never lived there except as an unhappy ghost."

"I'm not buying any," announced Judy. "I know when I've had enough."

Horace grinned, evidently feeling better.

"Well, ghost or no ghost, Lars Olsen had plenty of

reason to haunt the castle. My article will tell you more about it. You'll find it in my file under C if you want to refresh your memory."

"I do. I'd like to borrow it if I may."

Horace agreed to this, and Judy began searching through the filing cabinet that stood in one corner of his bedroom. He had copies of everything he had ever written neatly filed according to subject. Horace was nothing if not systematic.

"There's a lot my article doesn't tell," he admitted. "Maybe you and Peter can find out the truth about Emil Joerg. I couldn't. His name has gone down in county history as a crook and a swindler."

"And yet Olsen's daughter married him? Continue. This may be romantic as well as mysterious. Why was he called a swindler?"

"Lars Olsen bought fourteen thousand acres of land from Joerg and imported a colony of settlers. Work was nearly finished on the castle when it was discovered that Joerg didn't have a clear title to the land when he sold it. A trapper, Eleazer Dent by name, had staked out a previous claim—"

"And got the castle? But that doesn't seem fair," protested Judy.

"It didn't seem fair to a lot of people in old Eleazer's time, either. It was legal, though. Ask Peter."

Having studied and practiced law before joining the FBI, young Peter Dobbs was considered an authority, especially by Judy.

"I'm just filing it under V," Judy said

"What do you want to ask me?" Peter himself stood in the doorway. "I heard you were ill," he said to Horace. "What seems to be the trouble?"

"A virus—"

"I'm just filing it under V." Judy was standing before the filing cabinet with a manila folder in her hand. "Seriously," she said, "I'm borrowing Horace's article about the castle we're going to visit. It won't be as easy as we thought, Peter. The castle is inhabited."

"You don't say! Well, we'll see the inmates. What are they?" asked Peter. "A colony of ants?"

"No, they're people, and they don't like visitors. That sour-faced man we saw waiting in Dad's office is a sample. He guards the castle with his life."

Peter chuckled. "He does, does he? Well, he can't be guarding the castle and visiting his doctor at the same time. What's his name?"

"Bugs, Boggs—something like that. Mother told me, but I've forgotten."

"He isn't the owner," Horace put in. "John Dent, a descendant of the old trapper, owns the castle and probably employs this character as a caretaker or something. He shoos everyone away, saying the owner doesn't wish to be disturbed. That blue job out in front is probably John Dent's car."

"And John Dent is the owner? That's interesting," Judy said. "I wonder just *why* he doesn't wish to be disturbed."

CHAPTER II

The Unseen Violinist

"I HAVE a confession to make," Horace said as Judy and Peter were about to leave. "I haven't urged you to explore the mystery surrounding the castle, because I rather hoped to explore it myself."

Judy flashed her brother an encouraging smile.

"I suspected as much. Get well, and you can. In the meantime I'll find out about this birthday party."

"Do that," Horace said. "Find out as much as you can."

Peter did not ask about the birthday party until he and Judy had said good-bye to her parents and were on their way down the walk. The big blue car, they noticed, was still parked before the house.

"That would make a handsome present," he commented. "What were you saying about a birthday party? I thought we were on our way to explore a castle."

"We are," replied Judy, "if we can get in. With someone living there, it may not be easy unless we are invited to Mrs. Joerg's birthday party. It's soon. I don't know how soon, but she's going to be a hundred years old, so there ought to be quite a celebration. Maybe it will be held in the castle. It was built by her father, a famous violinist, but he lost it by not having a clear title to the land. That was something I wanted to ask you, Peter. If Lars Olsen lost his castle to Eleazer Dent, how could Olsen's daughter have been brought up there?"

"That is odd," Peter admitted. "Maybe Horace explains it in his article."

"I have it right here," Judy said, opening the folder. "I'll read it and see."

"Suppose you read it to me while I drive," Peter suggested. "Your father says I'm okay now. The bruised arm's as good as new."

"I'm glad."

Judy still felt a tightness in her throat when she thought of how Peter had been hurt and she hadn't been able to help him.

"Forget it," he said. "I've given you enough anxiety. Let's not lose each other in the castle, whatever we do."

"We'll stick together," promised Judy. "I won't even shut a door if you're on the other side of it. We've had enough. This castle hadn't better have a ghost. They always mean trouble."

"And you're always curious because you don't believe in them," Peter said teasingly.

It was true. Judy's natural curiosity had led her into most of her adventures. Even on her wedding day there had been the puzzle of the RAINBOW RIDDLE, followed by her weird experience when she hung the LIVING PORTRAIT in the house she had inherited from her grandmother. The old parlor bedroom of the house had been turned into Peter's office when he became resident agent for the FBI. Judy had worked right along with him on still more cases that aroused her curiosity. And now she was curious about the castle she and Peter were on their way to visit.

In the car Judy found her cat, Blackberry, sleeping on top of the back seat next to the rear window. Peter chuckled.

"Trust old Blackberry to find a comfortable spot for himself. He seems to take to the new car."

"He doesn't want to be left out of anything," Judy said as Peter started the motor.

Soon they were on their way out of the city of Farringdon on the familiar Roosevelt Highway. The morning air grew colder as they headed up into the mountains. Judy turned up the collar of her leopard coat.

"I'm glad I wore this," she said to Peter. "It makes me feel so luxurious, exactly like somebody on the way to visit a castle. Here's a picture of it, Peter."

"The coat?" he joked.

"No, silly, the castle. Mother was right about its being gloomy," Judy commented as she looked at the picture opposite Horace's article. "I wonder if it has a dungeon."

"Now what put that in your head?" asked Peter.

Judy said she didn't know. Castles were supposed to have dungeons, and old armor in unexpected corners, and all sorts of medieval furnishings. This one, she knew, was only a little more than a hundred years old, but it was probably a copy of some ancient castle.

In the picture it had four towers, two of them cracked as if by lightning. A wall with battlements along the top connected the towers and seemed to have but one great arched entrance. In the foreground most of the trees were as bare and grim as the castle itself. Judy shivered.

"Not a very cheerful place for the picnic we planned, is it?" she asked.

"The picture doesn't show the surrounding country," Peter reminded her. "We'll find a picnic place."

They turned up the road that used to be the old Jersey Shore Turnpike. "This was once a stage route, according to Horace's article," Judy said. "Wild tales of robberies and hold-ups are part of the region's folklore. I'm quoting Horace," she explained. "He says it was along this road that Lars Olsen's settlers laid a carpet of evergreen branches for his triumphant arrival on horseback. Afterwards, while they were celebrating, someone stole his horse!"

"Hijackers have taken the place of horse thieves," Peter declared. "Only last week a stolen seven- and a-half-ton truck was found abandoned along this road. Its cargo of woolens, naturally, was missing. But look, Judy. Can that be the castle?"

"Up there on the hilltop? Do you call that gray heap of rubble a castle?" asked Judy incredulously. "Why, there's nothing left of it but the wall and one tower. The picture shows four! Oh dear! It has changed a lot in a hundred years. But how do you get up to it? There doesn't seem to be any road."

Peter found a place to park the car, and Blackberry was out of it in a flash.

"Cats don't need roads. Why should we?" asked Peter.

"You're right," agreed Judy. "Cats can't read 'No Trespassing' signs either, and if anybody asks us why we are trespassing, we can simply explain that we're looking for our cat."

"We may end up doing just that. I don't see any road either," Peter said, taking Judy's arm, "but here's a little footpath. It must lead to the castle."

"I'm sure it does!" exclaimed Judy. "Don't you just *love* following a path?"

Peter's answer was a tender look that said more than words. Together they started up the path. At first, leaves rustled under their feet. Then they were walking on a soft carpet of pine needles. Suddenly the path turned and they could hear running water.

"A little waterfall! How lovely!"

Judy was enchanted. The path ran along beside the brook for a short distance above the waterfall and then zigzagged away from it. Another steep climb brought them abruptly to a stone wall. Peter stopped and listened.

"Do you hear what I hear?" he asked Judy.

"It isn't the waterfall. It's violin music!" she exclaimed. "And I'd swear it's coming from inside the castle!"

CHAPTER III

Two Little Spies

For some time Judy and Peter stood spellbound listening to the music. It was beautiful and yet, as she listened, a chill crept over Judy. She shivered in spite of the warmth of her leopard coat.

"Are you cold?" asked Peter.

"No," she replied. "It's the music. It gives me a creepy feeling. Look at this, Peter!" She spread the newspaper before him. "Horace says here in his article that 'Lars Olsen brought from his violin the rush and roar of rapid streams, the frolic of wind through leafy branches, and the tempest's crash on the mountain top.'"

"That sounds a bit wordy for a newspaper man," was Peter's comment.

16

"But don't you see?" cried Judy. "He was quoting from someone who had heard Lars Olsen play. And this music fits the description. You can hear it all, even the crash of the tempest! Who can it be?"

Peter grinned reassuringly.

"Certainly not Lars Olsen's ghost. The sound effects are the same, I'll admit, but it seems to me there's something besides the wind frolicking through the leafy branches over our heads. Listen! Don't you hear voices?"

Suddenly Judy and Peter were both listening. Not to the music any more—it had ceased as abruptly as it had begun. They were listening to voices that seemed to be coming from the tree right over their heads. A small boy's voice could now be heard distinctly.

"Keep watching like I told you."

"I am watching."

"Pretty soon the door will open. Then we'll know—"

"Know what, Emil?"

The girl's voice was hushed and expectant. Judy felt a shiver run down her spine as she listened. She moved closer to Peter. Blackberry, sensing her feelings as cats do, came from somewhere in the brush and began circling around them. Then he darted off. Where, they did not know. Up in the tree the boy was saying:

"If he's alive."

The girl's voice was now an excited whisper.

"We can't have the party in the castle if he isn't. Old Boggs would never let us in."

"*Mister* Boggs," the boy corrected her in a superior tone that reminded Judy of Horace and convinced her the two children must be brother and sister. "Granny says we're not to call him Old Boggs, because he's not old."

"I don't believe it," the girl said. "Anybody that cross has to be old, and I'm afraid of him. He said if we didn't stay away from here, something terrible would happen to us."

"What could he do?" scoffed the boy. "He doesn't own the castle. He's only the caretaker. Anyway, I saw him drive off in his car and he hasn't come back. This is our chance, Erna. If we're ever going to see what goes on in the castle, now is the time."

"I'm scared," Erna protested. "Granny thinks Uncle John is dead and they're not telling her. Do you think he is, Emil?"

"It wasn't in the papers."

"Maybe nobody knows it. Lots of things go on in the castle that nobody knows. The kids in school all say it's haunted, and I believe it."

Obviously, the two little spies were neighborhood children. They were hiding and watching the castle just as Judy herself would have liked to do. Hidden in the treetop, they undoubtedly had a good view of the great arched doorway that Judy had seen only in the picture. From where she stood she could see nothing but the one undamaged turret and the high stone wall.

"There! I see something moving," the boy, Emil, exclaimed excitedly. "There he is at the window! See, Erna! That's his black coat sleeve."

"There's *something* black." Erna's voice was suddenly disappointed. "Oh, Emil! It's only a big black cat."

"Blackberry!" Judy whispered, clutching at Peter's coat sleeve and, in her imagination, picturing vividly what the children had seen. "I might have known that cat would find his way inside the castle walls. I wonder—"

"Listen!" Peter interrupted.

"*Someone* was playing the violin," Emil was insisting. "And if Uncle John is dead, the way Granny says, it must be Grandpa Olsen's ghost."

"Did you hear that?" Judy whispered to Peter. "Let's find out who was playing. I'm curious, too."

"You would be. Well, here we go again," declared Peter, taking Judy's hand and helping her up the steep slope toward the castle. The path they were following now turned abruptly.

"This may lead to the great arched doorway you showed me in the picture," Peter was saying. "It's a little too steep—"

"Dead end," Judy interrupted.

They had come up against a high stone wall. There

were no stairs and certainly there was no door.

"We must have taken a wrong turn back there at the waterfall," Peter said. "We'll have to retrace our steps and try again. It's funny, though. A path usually leads somewhere."

"This one doesn't. It ends at the wall. Maybe people used to come here for picnics or something. You can see where they've carved their initials."

"So you can!"

Peter stopped to study the initials Judy pointed out. There were a number of them carved in the castle wall, chiseled deep in the stone and blackened by time.

"Look at this one, Peter!" Judy said. "It's a really old one, too. See, there's a heart with 'H. L.' and 'E. J.' carved in it. And here, right beside it, is another one with 'P. D.' and 'E. J.' Couldn't 'E. J.' make up his mind?"

"Some people can't," Peter remarked significantly, as they turned and walked back along the path.

"If you're teasing me," Judy said, her gray eyes serious, "I'm glad I couldn't until I'd grown up a little. Because it's wonderful when you are sure."

"It is, isn't it?" Peter's eyes smiled back at her.

A giggle from somewhere overhead spoiled their romantic mood. Judy and Peter were again under the tree where the children had been hiding and spying on the castle. Judy looked up. The tree overhead was a spreading oak with red leaves. The leaves rustled as if the children might be climbing still higher in the branches.

"They're out of sight," Judy reported. "I wonder how much of the castle they can see from where they are."

"Let's ask them. Hi, up there!" Peter called.

At first only an echo came back to him from the castle wall. Then a branch cracked and suddenly there was a crashing sound. Judy's heart almost stopped.

"They're falling!" she gasped. "Peter, you've startled the children and made them fall!"

CHAPTER IV

"Where Are They?"

MINUTES passed and nothing more happened. Judy was instantly sorry for having blamed Peter for the possible fate of the children and tried to tell him how she felt. But the words wouldn't come.

"I meant—I didn't mean—" she faltered.

"It's all right, Angel. Nothing happened. We won't startle them again," Peter promised. "They know we're here."

"They must have known it before you called," declared Judy, finding her voice.

"You're right," agreed Peter, "unless this is the Australian bush and that was a kookaburra laughing at us."

"A kooka what?" asked Judy.

"Burra," said Peter.

"Burr! I'm cold, too," giggled Judy.

"Those children must have been teasing us," Peter said. "Shall I call again?"

"Please do," begged Judy, "just to make sure they weren't hurt."

Judy looked up but still could see no trace of the children. Peter cupped his hands and called loudly:

"Hi, up there! Are you all right?"

Again there was a resounding echo, but no answer from the children.

"They must have climbed down when we weren't looking," concluded Judy. "Maybe they're on their way home. I think I know who they are."

"They mentioned Grandpa Olsen's ghost," recalled Peter. "Probably they're his great-great-grandchildren."

"If not his great-great-*great*-grandchildren. Oh, Peter!" exclaimed Judy. "Isn't it strange? Two children we could hear, but couldn't see, an invisible violinist, and the prospect of meeting an old lady a hundred years old. She must be the Granny the children were talking about. And they are planning a party in the castle. It was easier to find out about it than I thought it would be. But who is Uncle John?"

"Probably John Dent," Peter surmised. "He wouldn't be the children's real uncle, but they might call him that. If he actually is dead, there may be a mystery for us to solve, at that—"

Peter stopped as a rumbling sound was heard off to their left. "What was that?"

"It sounded like falling rock!" Judy said.

She listened, but heard nothing more. Then Blackberry appeared as if to explain it.

"Look at him! He's all dusty," observed Judy. "In attempting to scale the castle wall and get back to his master and mistress, he probably knocked loose a few stones."

Blackberry looked innocent, but they both knew he must have been the large black cat those two children had seen inside the castle walls. What had he discovered in there? How Judy wished he could talk!

"And now," she said, thinking aloud, "he knows what happened just now, while we can only guess."

"My guess would be that those children had something to do with it," Peter said.

"I didn't think of that. Oh dear!" lamented Judy. "Now I'm beginning to worry about them again. I did want to meet them. Their granny must be quite a character."

"Horace says the Joerg house is the next one down the road from the castle," Peter said. "Shall we go?"

Judy kept watching for the house through the trees as they went down another path that proved to be a short cut to the road. She was surprised when she saw what was hardly more than a shack surrounded by a number of tumble-down outbuildings. Only the barn had been painted.

"This must be the place," Peter said as they approached it.

"But it can't be," Judy objected. "The Joerg house would be a—a mansion, wouldn't it? Wait till you hear what Horace says in his article!"

The car was still parked where they had left it. They were walking toward the house, but now they stopped and Judy took the paper from the picnic basket Peter was carrying. She began to read:

"Emil Joerg is represented by his neighbors as having been a smooth-tongued swindler, wholly unworthy of confidence and thoroughly detested by everyone who knew him. Hilma Olsen married him only after a bitter quarrel with the Dent family, each accusing the other of swindling her father out of his fortune."

"I don't quite get it," Peter said. "Where does the Dent family come in?"

"They brought her up. It says here somewhere that after Lars Olsen's death his daughter, Hilma, was raised by the Dent family, who moved into the castle. They had three children, and a fourth child, John Dent, was born in the castle and still lives there as a recluse. We hope," Judy added.

"The old lady may be right," declared Peter. "Look at this!"

Horace's article continued:

Nobody has been seen at the castle in recent years except the caretaker, Hiram Boggs, who told this reporter that the feud between the two families was never settled. Apparently, no attempt has been made to restore the castle. Only a part of it remains standing, two of the towers having been struck by lightning in the days when misfortune seemed to follow Lars Olsen at every step. What happened to the eighty thousand dollars purchase money is still a mystery.

"It doesn't look as if the Joergs had any of it, if they live here," commented Judy when she had finished reading.

Peter shook his head.

"It beats me! The Dents haven't spent any of it either. From what we could see of the castle, it's hardly fit to live in."

"It's a puzzle, all right," agreed Judy.

The name "Joerg" on the mailbox told her there was no mistake, and yet she felt that there must be a mistake somewhere.

"Wait!" she said to Peter. "Let's decide what questions we're going to ask, before we go in. I am curious, but it would be unkind to pry. Shall we say we're from the *Herald?* We are supposed to be doing this for Horace and yet, somehow, I don't think the Joergs want any more publicity. I don't think—"

She stopped. What she didn't think suddenly became unimportant. The door had opened.

CHAPTER V

Grandmother Joerg

It was a young woman who opened the door. Judy's surprise must have shown in her face. She had expected Grandmother Joerg to open the door and then slam it in her face the way she had done when Horace called to interview her.

The young woman smiled and stepped outside.

"Are you looking for someone?" she asked, and her voice was pleasant. Everything about her was pleasant, and this was unexpected, too. Before either Judy or Peter could answer, she said, "I am. I'm looking for my twins. Maybe you've seen them. They're dressed alike in blue jeans and red corduroy jackets. They'll be ten their next birthday, but they're small for their age. They have straight blond hair, cut short, and their eyes are blue."

"That sounds like a police description," Peter said, grinning in the boyish way Judy loved. "Have they been missing long?"

The young woman laughed apologetically.

"I'm sorry," she said. "I suppose I am a little over-anxious about them but, you see, they're all we have. They've only been gone since breakfast. It's time for their lunch now. I thought you might have seen them."

"Are their names Emil and Erna?" asked Judy. "I guessed they were brother and sister, but I didn't know they were twins."

"But anyone would know." She seemed puzzled. "I forgot to tell you their names, of all things, after telling you so much else about them. How did you find out what their names were?"

"That's easy! We heard them," Peter replied, "when they called each other by name. You're Mrs. Joerg, aren't you?"

"Yes. I'm their mother," the woman explained. "My husband's great-grandmother is Mrs. Joerg, too. She worries when the twins don't come home on time. They're forbidden to play near the castle, and yet they will go there. Is that where they were?"

"I'm afraid it is, Mrs. Joerg."

"They had climbed a tree in order to see over the castle wall," Judy explained. "We didn't see them, but we did hear them talking."

"About the castle ghost, I suppose? Nobody knows how these rumors start, but once children get hold of them they spread like the measles, and I'm afraid my two do their share of the spreading. I don't usually talk to strangers myself," the twins' mother continued, smiling. "You never know who is from the papers and who isn't. There was quite a story in the *Farringdon Daily Herald* about a year ago, and ever since then people have been driving by, like you two, on purpose to see the castle. I suppose that is why you're here."

"It is," Judy admitted. "We brought a picnic lunch."

"It's a little late in the season for picnics, isn't it?"

"My wife doesn't think so."

Judy loved the way Peter said "my wife." It was all the introduction Mrs. Joerg seemed to want.

"You can picnic on our property if you like," she said. "We own the land below the castle wall. You can't make a mistake. John Dent's got 'No Trespassing' signs posted all over his property, and that caretaker, Hiram Boggs, makes sure that nobody does trespass. The children can't understand it. They can remember a time when they were welcome to visit the castle."

"They were?" Judy was thinking of the feud that reportedly had never been settled.

"Of course," Mrs. Joerg said. "Does that seem strange to you?"

"A little," Judy admitted. "There are so many stories."

Mrs. Joerg laughed. "If you read the one that was

in the *Herald* you probably got the idea there was an old feud between the two families. But that's not true. Granny, as we call her, was brought up by the Dents. John is like her own brother."

"How long has it been since you've seen him?" Peter asked.

"Granny could tell you. They had words a couple of years ago. The neighbors started talk of a family feud all over again. These 'No Trespassing' signs were posted and the children were chased away every time they went near the castle. If you see them—"

"Tell 'em to git home fast or their granny will take a stick to them and she's well able to," rasped the voice of a bent old lady who came hobbling around the corner of the house at that moment. She carried a crooked stick, and a fat old goose waddled along in front of her. Judy tried not to stare. But the old lady reminded her so much of pictures she had seen of Mother Goose that it was difficult not to gaze at her in awe and wonder. Her face was criss-crossed with wrinkles, but her eyes were bright and sharp.

"This is Granny," young Mrs. Joerg said to Judy and Peter. "That's Florabelle, her pet goose. Granny will be a hundred years old the day after tomorrow, but she's out every day looking after her pets. She even splits kindling for the stove, don't you, Granny?"

"You bet I do. In my day," the old lady said, "a woman had to work if she wanted to live. I don't

The old lady reminded Judy of Mother Goose

mean Emil wasn't good to me, God rest his soul, but we both had it hard what with the neighbors all against us and nobody willing to give Emil a job with their talk of the money he held back from my father. Well, I want to tell you right now, he gave back every dollar. He swore he would and you can come in and see for yourselves, we ain't had any of it to spend."

Judy and Peter were struck speechless. Was this an invitation to enter the house, or wasn't it? Again Judy felt a reluctance to pry.

"Well, come in! Not you, Florabelle!" Granny Joerg swung her stick at the goose, which had started to follow her into the house. "If you're sightseers you might as well come in and take in the sights, and if you're from the newspapers you can tell them, if they want the truth—"

"But, Granny," the young Mrs. Joerg protested. "Who knows the truth? There are so many stories and there's no way of proving which one is true. Besides, these young people may not be interested in any of them."

"Then why are they snooping around here?" snapped the old lady.

Judy was seized with an inspiration.

"Maybe we want your recipe for a long life, Mrs. Joerg."

"So that's it! Hard work and someone to care about besides yourself. That's my recipe." She gave an ancient cackle. "I thought you were from the papers. Come to report my birthday, eh? Well, if you see that the truth's told, you may get an invitation."

"We'll report nothing but the truth," declared Judy. "Anything you tell us will be printed word for word as you said it."

"Come in then." Young Mrs. Joerg held the door open. Feeling like a reporter, Judy had her pad and pencil ready the moment she and Peter entered the house.

CHAPTER VI

A Haunting Picture

THERE was something homelike about the room they entered even though it was without most of the comforts of modern living. The furniture consisted of a round golden oak table and a few assorted chairs. An old-fashioned treadle sewing machine like the one Judy's grandmother used to own was still in use, and a tall china closet filled with everything from dishes to the children's toys stood against one wall. There were rag rugs on the floor, and the room was heated by an ancient wood stove with a pan in front to catch the ashes. A kettle of potato soup bubbled on top and a fire glowed inside.

"It's nice and warm in here," Judy commented, not knowing what else to say.

"Those old boxes I chopped up make good firewood," chuckled Granny. "They spark a little, though, and they do heat up the room. You have to watch them with this old stove. Well, take off your things and sit a spell. Maybe you'd like to look at some pictures."

"Indeed we would. We were going to ask you for one of yours," began Peter. "The paper would probably be glad to send a photographer—"

"To take a picture of this wrinkled old face? No, thank you," Granny said. "I know I ain't much to look at any more. There was a time when I was proud to have my picture taken, though. I wasn't bad looking when I was a girl."

She hobbled over to the china closet and returned with an open album.

"There I am," she said, pointing a bony finger at a faded photograph. It showed a delicate young girl seated in an ornate chair. She was pretty. But it was the man standing beside her who captured Judy's attention when she looked at the picture. Underneath it he had written in the flowery handwriting that was popular in his day:

Sincerely,
Lars Olsen and daughter Hilma

The girl was like her father except that his mouth curved upward in a wistful half smile and his eyes were larger and more dreamy. They seemed to be looking off somewhere toward a distant vision.

It was a haunting picture. Had Lars Olsen been dreaming of his castle when it was taken? There was something of sadness in his face, too, as if he knew somehow that his dream would never be fully realized.

"Olsen's castle in the air, they called it."

Judy gave a start. It was Granny Joerg speaking almost as though she had read Judy's thoughts.

"He wanted it for his children and grandchildren and great-grandchildren. But it's brought them nothing but trouble," Granny was saying, "and I have a premonition that there's more to come."

"Don't say that, Granny!"

Young Mrs. Joerg turned an anxious face toward Judy and Peter. "Too often Granny's premonitions turn out to be true. There's this premonition about John Dent, for instance."

"He's dead," Granny said. "I feel it in my bones. He said to me, 'Hilma, if you live to be a hundred, we'll have a big celebration at the castle.' There won't be much of a party unless he keeps his word, and he can't if he's dead, now can he?"

"If he's dead," Peter said, "there has to be a record—"

"Unless Hiram Boggs kept it secret. It would mean the loss of his job. Deborah's folks wouldn't keep him on as caretaker. They'd sell the castle if it went to them. Maybe offer it to the state for a park."

"I see. Who is Deborah?"

Peter glanced at Judy, who was busy taking notes.

"One of the Dent girls," replied Granny. "There were three of them—Flora, Priscilla, and Deborah. They're all dead now. Debbie was the only one who left any descendants. They live in upstate New York some place. Name's Tinkle."

"Tinkle?"

"Finkle? Tinkle? Something like that. I never could get it straight. We used to call him Mr. Twinkle when he was courtin' Debbie. The Dents had the castle fixed up real nice. That is, the east tower. They never got around to the others. Lightning struck two of them."

"But the east tower was furnished?"

"Oh, yes! Velvets, tapestries, everything like that. There was a suit of armor, I remember, used to stand in one corner of the big entrance hall. I'd like to see it once more."

"You will," Peter said.

That sounded like a promise. Judy knew Peter would keep it if he could. He didn't make promises recklessly. But would she see the castle? Somehow, the party had to be there.

"This recipe," Judy said. "I want to be sure I have it right. You said hard work and someone to care about besides yourself?"

"I mean my family. I can still do for them. There's my grandson's boy, Emil, and my great-great-grandson. He's called Emil, too," the old lady explained. "It's a good name and one my boys ought to be proud of. If you could clear it of scandal, I'd be real grateful. A good word in the papers . . ."

Her voice trailed off as if she were suddenly tired of talking.

"We'll try," Judy promised. "We're gathering the facts for my brother. We aren't really reporters, but we'll do our best."

"Nobody can do better 'n that," Granny replied. "I done my best, too, but maybe it wasn't good enough. My father was a fine man and deserved better than he got. He fell off the wall, you know, and was killed. Little Emil should have been called Lars, maybe. Every time I look in his face I see my father's eyes looking back at me. Erna, too. They're beautiful children. You can see for yourselves what a resemblance there is."

"But Granny," remarked young Mrs. Joerg, taking the album to put it away again, "they tell me they didn't see the children. They only heard them talking in a tree—"

"A tree! May the Lord help them!" exclaimed the old lady. "Is it the tree that leans over the castle wall?"

"Does it?"

Judy and Peter were both asking the question. They hadn't noticed that the tree leaned over the wall, but perhaps it did.

"Something must be keeping the twins," declared their mother. "They are never this late for their lunch. It's after one o'clock. I do wish you'd hurry right back and warn them—"

"Of what?" asked Judy. "What is the danger?"

"We don't know," young Mrs. Joerg admitted. "I don't trust that Hiram Boggs, that's all. Oh, if you could find out what goes on in the castle without making everything public—"

"We could and we will," promised Peter, "and if we see the children we'll tell them to hurry home."

As they were leaving the house, Blackberry darted out from behind a clump of bushes near the entrance. Waving his tail gently, he strolled after Judy and Peter.

"Let's look for the children in the tree and then eat our lunch by the wall where those initials are," Judy suggested as Peter hurried her back along the path they had taken down from the castle.

"Initials?" asked Peter, his thoughts, apparently, on something else.

The morning had given them both a great deal to think about. Should they have investigated that crash like falling rock? Suppose the children had fallen! Judy remembered, with a shudder, that Lars Olsen had been killed when he fell from the castle wall. Was it the wall with the carved initials? They wouldn't have been there then. Or would they?

"Peter!" Judy said suddenly. "I think I've figured out whose initials they were."

"You have?"

Now he was really listening.

"Yes, it just came to me," she replied. "H. L. was Granny herself, and E. J. simply has to be Emil Joerg."

"It makes sense," agreed Peter. "Hilma Larsen and Emil Joerg, but who was P. D.?"

"One of the Dent girls, probably. Wasn't there a Priscilla who never married? She could have started the story that Emil Joerg was a swindler. I mean if she and Granny were both in love with him and she wanted to get even——"

"There are a lot of *ifs* in that story," Peter interrupted. "Too many to suit me. Let's take a look at the facts. For instance, it's fact and not conjecture that none of Lars Olsen's purchase money was spent on the Joerg house."

"What do you think happened to it, Peter? No money was spent on the castle, either. Look at it up there on the hill ahead! It's practically in ruins."

"We haven't seen the inside of it yet."

"We will," Judy predicted. "Granny Joerg spoke as if considerable money had been spent on it when she was living there. Maybe the Dents took her in to salve their consciences after her father died. Maybe——"

"Wait a minute!" Peter stopped her. "That's the way these stories spread. Someone says maybe something happened and it's repeated as if it had happened and so it goes. A story could grow considerably over a hundred years."

"I know," Judy said, "and this one probably has. I'm afraid Horace's article only revived tales that might better have been forgotten—"

"Or disproved."

"You're right, Peter," declared Judy, "and we're just the ones to disprove them. I feel sorry for the Joergs. Wouldn't it be wonderful if we could find out the truth about that purchase money people said they kept? Something must have happened to it. Eighty thousand dollars couldn't vanish into thin air."

"Was it that much?" asked Peter.

"Horace says so in his article. Emil Joerg's story was that he gave it to Lars Olsen, who then left to call on the Dents, who had already moved into the castle. Olsen never arrived, and when he was found dead he had no money on him. Horace doesn't say who found him. I wonder if he knows. Peter, I was just thinking. Lars Olsen may have taken this path to the castle."

"But this path leads to a blank wall," Peter objected.

"That's it! Oh, Peter, that's it!" Judy cried, suddenly excited.

CHAPTER VII

Below the Wall

"Now what?" Peter asked. "Have you forgotten we're supposed to be looking for the twins? Though we seem to be up against a blank wall there, ourselves."

"That's what I mean," explained Judy. "This path can't lead to a blank wall. It just appears to. They may have followed it to where it really leads."

Peter gave up. Judy could tell by the look he gave her. She couldn't explain her own sudden feeling that the path did lead somewhere. Always, in her dreams, when she followed a path it led to an open door. And when she opened that door it led to another and another. Judy loved her dreams of doors that opened.

Sometimes they would be hidden in closets or behind furniture. Even trees had opened for her. So why not a wall? The children would understand if she could find them.

"You know, Peter," she said, "I know exactly the way those children must feel about the castle. They've probably heard all these rumors about it and are just as eager to find out the truth as we are."

"Then they may be in trouble," he said, frowning.

"Why do you say that?" Judy asked.

"You're comparing them with us," Peter chuckled, "and we manage to get ourselves in trouble occasionally."

"Occasionally? You mean constantly! Maybe we ought to call them," Judy suggested.

"Emil! Erna!" they both shouted. "Your granny says to hurry right home. Lunch is ready!"

When the echo had died away, Peter said, "That reminds me. Is there anything good in this picnic basket I'm carrying? I could eat a horse."

"Sorry, I didn't pack a horse," Judy said.

She had meant to be funny, but Peter didn't laugh.

"I guess it was a pretty corny joke," she admitted. "I'm hungry, too, but do let's find those children first."

They followed the path for a little while in silence. When they came to the tree where the children had been hiding before, they called again, and again there was an answering echo.

"They aren't up there any more," Peter said. "They would have answered us."

"Would they?" asked Judy. "They saw us the other time and giggled, but they wouldn't answer when we called. Maybe they don't want us to know where they are. I'm tempted to climb the tree myself and look for them. They must have had a good view of the castle from the way they were talking. If I tell them we're willing to help them with the birthday—"

"Listen!" Peter interrupted. "I did hear an answer. It sounded as if it came from behind the castle wall."

"But it's the wall that throws back the echo," Judy objected.

"This wasn't an echo."

"Are you certain, Peter?"

"Let's call again to make sure," he suggested.

They called a third time.

"Emil! Erna! You're wanted at home!"

"*Ome!*" came back from the castle walls, and this time both Judy and Peter knew it was only the echo of their own voices. Judy shivered.

"I don't like it," she said. "It makes the castle seem alive. Peter, I'm still determined to see inside those walls. If the children could climb this tree and spy on the castle, why couldn't we? I'm going to try it."

"In your fur coat?"

Removing her coat and hanging it on a convenient bush, Judy put on the sweater that had served as a

cover for the picnic basket. She was glad she had been
sensible enough to wear slacks. All the adventures of
the small redheaded tomboy she used to be came back
to her as she swung herself over the first branch of
the tree.

"You see, I haven't lost my skill," she called down
to Peter. "Remember when we used to climb trees
together in Grandma's grove—ours now? This is fun!
Now I can see the Joerg house. There's nobody in the
yard now. Granny and young Mrs. Joerg must have
gone inside."

"Then perhaps I did make a mistake," Peter said.
"If they've gone inside, the children probably have
come home to lunch and there's nothing more for us
to worry about."

"No? What about John Dent? I would certainly
like to know whether he's dead or alive, wouldn't
you?"

Judy didn't hear Peter's answer because, at that
moment, the branch on which she was standing gave a
warning snap and she had to catch hold of another
branch higher up.

"Are you all right?" Peter asked.

"All right now," Judy reassured him. "I nearly fell,
though. The long branch that leans over the castle wall is broken, but there are other branches
higher up."

"Be careful, Angel," warned Peter.

Judy felt that the nickname fitted her for once as she continued to climb toward the bluest sky she had ever seen. She could see it through the flaming foliage of the tree, but in the west a dark storm cloud was rapidly covering it. The sun, shining behind the cloud, lined it with silver.

"It doesn't look real," thought Judy.

Just as she had hoped, she had a splendid view of the castle and all the surrounding hills from the top of the tree.

"See anything more?" Peter shouted up to her.

"I can see everything!" she exclaimed. "Imagine, Peter, there are chickens in the castle yard! I don't see any people, though. It's just like anybody's yard, not even very pretty, but the hills and the sky with those broken turrets against it are beautiful. I can see all over."

Judy was so enchanted by what she saw that Peter had to climb up before she would come down. He viewed all the splendor, but made no comment until they were on solid ground again. Then he said, "Whew! I thought I'd never get you down from there, Angel. We had a glimpse of heaven, all right. But did you see the children?"

"Not a trace of them," Judy replied, "but I did see that big arched doorway. There's a road leading to it and a car parked beside the road."

"A blue car? I saw it, too."

"It looks as if Hiram Boggs is back again, guarding the castle, doesn't it? The children are afraid of him. Maybe he chased them home."

"I don't think so. We didn't meet them along the path," Peter objected.

"There were a lot of paths branching off in different directions back by the waterfall," Judy remembered, "and there's the main road where our car is parked, too. How do we know the children didn't go home another way?"

"We don't, but perhaps we better find out."

"Peter!" Judy broke in suddenly. "What's that shiny thing beside the path? Is it a penny?"

Peter gave a low whistle of surprise.

"You'd soon be rich if you found many pennies like this!" he exclaimed as he picked up the shiny coin.

Judy saw now that it was smaller than a penny. It was even smaller and thinner than a dime and it looked as if it were made of pure gold.

"Is it real money?" she asked.

"It sure is," he replied. "It's a gold dollar. We'll try and find out who lost it, but right now let's keep it for luck. We still have those twins to find."

CHAPTER VIII

Another Discovery

PETER wrapped the tiny gold coin in a piece of notebook paper and put it in his pocket. Judy had never seen a gold dollar before and fully intended to look at it later under a magnifying glass and learn the date. Right now she was more interested in finding the Joerg twins.

"Peter," she asked after a moment, "do you still think you heard those children behind the castle wall?"

"I thought I did. But you just about talked me out of it," he admitted. "I thought I heard the little girl crying."

"Behind the wall?"

"The sound did seem to come from there. It was very indistinct."

"That's strange," Judy said. "We both thought we heard violin music, but maybe that was an echo from somewhere, too. The other time, I didn't hear a thing."

"You didn't? Well, let's listen again."

Judy and Peter both stood perfectly still and listened again without calling. The wind made an eerie whistling sound, and somewhere a bird was singing. But that was all they heard.

"I don't hear anything now except the wind," Peter said. "I think a storm is blowing up. It's growing colder by the minute."

"It's the chill around this gloomy old castle," declared Judy. "Let's listen again close to the wall. If there is someone crying behind it—"

A twig snapped.

"Now there's someone off in the other direction. Or is that only Blackberry?"

"Why not call him and find out?" Peter suggested.

Judy began to call, "Here, kitty, kitty, kitty!" the way she always did when she had food for her pet.

Almost immediately Blackberry was arching his back and purring around her. But he had come from still another direction. Judy rewarded him with a small piece of liverwurst from the picnic basket Peter was carrying.

"Don't I get any reward?" Peter asked plaintively. "I come when you call me, too."

"Isn't that gold dollar you pocketed reward enough?" asked Judy, laughing.

When Peter reminded her that he couldn't eat it, she had to give in to him. They each took a sandwich from the top of the basket but continued searching for the twins as they ate. They edged along the castle wall as far as they could go beyond the end of the path and then, finding the way blocked by a pile of rubble, started back.

"Here are those initials again," Peter said. "I'll carve ours just below them on this smooth stone—"

"Peter! Watch out!" cried Judy. "That stone is loose."

"So it is!" he exclaimed. "Look at this, Judy! What do you know about that!"

He removed the stone, and there behind it was a deep hiding place. Judy's first thought was that something surely had been hidden there. Then it entered her mind that she had been right about the path leading to a door in the wall. There seemed to be a wooden panel at the back.

"There must have been a door there when the castle was first built, and then it was closed off for some reason," she began.

"What reason?" asked Peter.

"I can't think of one at the moment," replied Judy. "Maybe this is like my dream castle with doors that lead to other doors in all sorts of unexpected places. The children couldn't have gone in this way, could they?"

"Not unless they reduced themselves to the size of dolls. I don't suppose the door behind the wall still opens, but we could push against it and see."

"Let me," Judy offered. "My hands are smaller."

She thrust them both inside the opening and pushed with all her might, but nothing happened. Then Peter tried it.

"If it is a door, it must be locked," he said at last. "Probably it has been locked for a long, long time."

"Since Lars Olsen locked it, probably. He must have known it was there, because he built the castle—"

"But this is Emil Joerg's property below the wall," Peter broke in thoughtfully.

"That's right!" exclaimed Judy. "And those *are* his initials on the rock."

"Yes, go on! That makes sense."

But Judy had stopped to study the initials more closely.

"Peter, look at this!" she pointed out. "Do you see that arrow through the heart where those initials are carved? It points to the stone we just removed. I do believe it was meant to. Something must have been hidden behind that stone!"

"It's like finding a treasure map," he agreed, and there was awe in his voice. "Whatever was hidden here may have been removed just recently. I'm not just guessing. See that little shoe print? There's another and another! They were both here. No wonder they were

"Let me up! I can explain everything."

late for lunch. They'll have a very good excuse—"

"Wait!" Judy stopped him. "This time I do hear something. Another twig snapped. Someone is watching us from over there in the bushes where I hung my coat."

"Can it be the children?"

"I don't know," Judy said.

Suddenly, without knowing why, she was afraid. She moved closer to Peter and began to shiver.

"You need your coat," he said. "I'll get it for you if you'll show me the bush—"

"There!" Judy pointed. Then she gasped. "It *was* there, on that bush with the red leaves. Oh, Peter! It's gone! My beautiful leopard coat that you gave me for Christmas! Why was I ever foolish enough to wear it on a picnic? Now it's gone!"

"It probably hasn't gone very far," Peter said. "That bush is still moving. Someone is hiding behind it."

"Stop him, Peter!"

Even as Judy spoke, Peter dived into the bushes. Hurling himself upon the figure who crouched there, he retrieved Judy's coat and tossed it to her.

"How's that for fast action?" he asked.

His FBI training had made him quick and sure. Judy could not see the thief he had pinned to the ground, but she could hear him pleading, "Let me up! I can explain everything."

"Everything?" asked Peter in a tone Judy had seldom heard him use. "Then you'd better begin by explaining what you intended to do with that coat."

"I intended to find out who left it there," the man whined. "Isn't that what you would do if you found a fur coat hanging on a bush?"

The humor of the situation must have struck Peter, for he laughed and admitted that it probably was.

"How," he asked, "were you going to find out?"

The thief did not have a ready answer for that one. Judy could see Peter regarding him suspiciously.

"Who is he?" she wondered.

She could see only the back of the man who had been hiding in the bushes. He had straightened to his full height, but still he lacked six inches or so of being as tall as Peter. He was stockier, though. His graying hair told Judy he was not a young man.

"John Dent!" thought Judy.

For a moment she felt certain he must be the castle recluse. Then he turned around.

CHAPTER IX

Mr. Boggs Explains

"Why, Peter, it's Mr. Boggs," Judy exclaimed, coming closer. "Did you tell him we have Mrs. Joerg's permission to picnic here? We aren't trespassing."

"No, but Mr. Boggs is."

"Me?" asked the man in apparent surprise.

"Yes, you," replied Peter. "I understand this land belongs to the Joergs. Perhaps you would like to explain what you are doing here."

"It was those Joerg twins," the caretaker answered. "They're always up to something. Climbed a tree and slid down a broken branch into the castle yard, but I caught them and chased them home. Then, when I heard you two young folks, I said to myself, 'They've sneaked back here. That's what they've done.' So I ducked behind the bushes to watch for them—"

"And took my coat with you?"

"Just for safekeeping. I had no idea who left it there until this young man jumped me."

"You were a little rough on him, Peter," Judy said.

"My apologies, if your intentions were innocent. By the way, Mr. Boggs, what time was it when you sent the children home?" Peter asked.

"Let me see, it must have been about a half an hour ago, maybe a little more. I heard somebody calling them—"

"Us," Judy whispered.

"Did you hear the children answer?" questioned Peter.

"I wasn't sure. Maybe they did. This castle wall throws back an echo and it's hard to tell. They were running down the road toward home the last I saw of them."

"The main road?" asked Judy.

Mr. Boggs nodded.

"Then I was right, Peter!"

Judy couldn't help feeling elated about it. Sometimes she liked to win an argument, too. She liked to show Peter that she had just as logical a mind as he did, even if he was a trained federal agent.

"You did imagine that crying," she added. "It was just the echo of our own voices when we called. It's nice to know the children are safe at home, isn't it?"

"If they are safe," Peter said, as though there was still some doubt of it, "I suppose it would be foolish to keep on searching for them."

"Granny Joerg asked us to send them home," Judy explained to Mr. Boggs. "She doesn't want them to play near the castle."

"Humph! That's what she tells you. In my opinion she's the one who sends them here," Mr. Boggs declared. "That old lady is a sly one. Probably sent you here to stir up more trouble. If you had come around to the main gate, I could have told you the children were on their way home. I threatened them with a stick. That sends them scurrying. Otherwise they'd be hanging around here most of the time, trying to get a glimpse of their uncle John, as they call him. He's a cripple, you know."

"No, I didn't know," Judy said in surprise.

"Your father knows. You're Dr. Bolton's daughter, aren't you? He told me who you were this morning when I saw him. And this young man is your husband, I understand. What does he do for a living?"

"He studied law," Judy answered quickly, not mentioning Peter's connection with the FBI.

"Law, eh?" The caretaker of the castle looked at Peter sharply. "There was quite a legal squabble over the land Lars Olsen bought when he built his castle. Emil Joerg sold it to him without knowing Eleazer

Dent had already staked out a claim. Olsen must have seen the stakes, though. He built the castle wall right on the line. In fact, it juts over on the Joerg property a foot or more and there was a row over that, too. The Joergs say they can cart away the stones whenever they feel like it. You interested in that?"

"Very much so," replied Peter. "We noticed the stones were loose in some places. We heard violin music and what I thought was someone crying behind the wall. Can you explain that, Mr. Boggs?"

"There are some things that can't be explained," the man replied in a lowered voice. "They don't bother me, of course, but there are people who say Lars Olsen comes back here and plays his violin to torment John Dent, who robbed him of his money—"

"Now, wait a minute," Peter stopped him. "Unless I'm mistaken in my dates, John Dent was only a baby when Lars Olsen died—"

"Or was killed. Some say robbery was the motive."

"It might very well have been," Peter admitted, "but when you accuse a two-year-old baby of the crime, I think you're carrying it a little too far."

"Maybe I don't have any facts to back up what I say," the caretaker returned stubbornly. "But John Dent's got the money, if you want my opinion."

"But you haven't any facts?"

"Well, that depends." Mr. Boggs looked at Peter as if he were trying to figure him out. "Course, I shouldn't talk against him, working for him like I do. He pays me well, even lets me use his car. It's no good to him as he never leaves the castle and won't let a soul except his doctor in to see him."

"His doctor?" Judy questioned. "That's my father, isn't it?"

"Was," Boggs said. "He switched to a younger man who doesn't know his business. That's what I went to see your father about this morning. The prescription he gave him helped him more than all the medicine this young doc has prescribed, but the druggist wouldn't refill it without your father's written orders. Ask him about it yourself. He'll tell you."

"I'll do that," Judy said.

She looked at Peter, who had the strangest expression on his face. He glared at the man's back as he turned and went off toward the castle. The sky had suddenly darkened. Judy felt the first drop of rain splash on her nose.

"Oh dear! That spoils our picnic!" she exclaimed.

"It sure does," Peter agreed. But from his tone of voice Judy knew he didn't mean the rain.

"We can eat in the car," Judy said cheerfully. "And look at all we found out!" she added. "Here we were worrying over a hundred questions, when all we had to do was ask Mr. Boggs. I thought he was pretty nice after the way you knocked him over and pinned him to the ground."

"He was too nice," declared Peter. "I don't trust him."

"You mean you think he really was trying to steal my coat? It feels good now," Judy added as she pulled up the collar. "It's growing colder by the minute."

"Even the weather is against us," observed Peter. "This rain is turning to hail."

"Blackberry doesn't know what to make of it. Look at him!" Judy exclaimed.

The cat's ears were flattened back as if he were angry at the sky for playing such a trick on him. He shook the hail from his coat with an air of injured dignity and then darted ahead of Judy and Peter as they hurried down the path toward the car.

CHAPTER X

Questions

"It's still here, Peter!"

They had reached the road and Judy was looking at the car through the pelting hail almost as if she hadn't expected to find it there.

Peter laughed. "Did you think it wouldn't be?"

"I don't know," she replied. "Everything has been so strange today. I guess I haven't finished sorting out my thoughts."

"Want to drive down and check with the Joergs just to make sure the children are all right, before we head for home?" Peter asked.

"I'd rather go right home and find out what Dad has to tell us," Judy admitted.

Blackberry was the first one in when Peter opened the car door. He leaped up on the back seat and from there to his favorite place beside the rear window, as Peter started the motor.

Somehow, Judy got the impression Peter had given in to her against his own judgment, and she didn't want that. They rode for a little while in silence except for the slipping sound of the windshield wiper against the glass. Then Judy asked, "Want another sandwich while you're driving?"

Peter shook his head. Something was worrying him, Judy knew. The picnic basket was still filled with food, but she wasn't hungry for it, either. The rain pelted down steadily as Peter guided the car along the slippery road. Judy had a last look at the castle as they rounded the bend.

"I wonder," she said, and left the sentence half finished.

"So do I," agreed Peter. "There must be some way we can find out the truth about John Dent. I still think the man may be dead."

"You do?" Judy was surprised to hear this. "I'll ask Dad what he knows and if it doesn't check with what Mr. Boggs told us, we'll come back and really investigate. I would like to explore that castle just for fun."

"If we explore it," Peter said, "it won't be just for fun."

He looked so grim that Judy changed the subject.

They stopped as soon as the rain let up a little and finished the sandwiches Judy had packed and drank all the coffee in the thermos jug.

"I needed that coffee to take the chill out of my bones," declared Judy. "That gray old ruin up there on the hilltop gives me the shivers. If John Dent isn't dead, he might just as well be. I wouldn't call it living to be shut away from everybody in that gloomy retreat. I like my dream castle a lot better."

"Your dream castle?" asked Peter. "It isn't the Farringdon-Pett place, is it? I always knew that old house with turrets like a castle appealed to you, but you never told me you dreamed about it."

"I didn't," Judy said. "This was our own house in Dry Brook Hollow. I dreamed I opened a closet to clean it and there was a little door that led to another and another. I dream it over and over, only to find the doors in all sorts of different places. Once I found one in a tree."

"And once," continued Peter, "you found one in a stone wall, only it wasn't a dream."

As they turned off the old Jersey Shore Turnpike and drove back along the main road through the rain, they speculated about what might be behind the door they had found.

By the time they reached Farringdon it had stopped raining and Judy was beginning to feel sorry they had left the castle without doing some more exploring.

"But how could we?" she asked later, when she had told Horace all about their adventure.

He was up, and said he was feeling much better.

"In fact, I may be well enough to go to that birthday party with you," he said. "I wouldn't want to miss it if it's going to be held in the castle. It seems to me it would bring a little life into John Dent's lonely existence to have it there."

"The children were planning it," Judy recalled as she thought back over the events of the day.

Somewhere in the back of her mind she discovered a nagging worry that was not relieved by Horace's asking: "What happened to those children?"

Judy looked at Peter and realized, since she'd been the one to decide not to stop off at the Joergs' to see if the children had reached home safely, she'd have to do the explaining. It wasn't going to be easy.

"Well," she began, "they broke a branch of a tree and slid down it, and when Mr. Boggs found them inside the castle wall he chased them home."

"But you didn't meet them on that path you took?"

"No, they went around by the road."

"How do you know?" asked Horace.

This last question hit Judy hard. She turned to Peter, who had been listening but not saying anything.

"Peter, how do we know?"

"We don't," he said shortly. "We just took Mr. Boggs' word for it. If he lied—"

"Oh, Peter! Suppose he did! That's what you were

worrying about all the way home, wasn't it?" asked
Judy. "We should have gone back to the house and
checked with Mrs. Joerg."

"Let's check with your father first," Peter suggested
as Dr. Bolton was heard ascending the stairs.

"What's this?" asked Dr. Bolton, regarding the
three in the room first with interest and then with dis-
approval as his gaze rested upon Horace. "Son, you're
supposed to be in bed if you still have fever."

"I haven't, Dad. I feel as good as new," declared
Horace. "Your medicine did its work fast."

"Speaking of medicine—"

"We were speaking of it, Dad," Judy told him. "I
don't usually ask questions about your patients. I know
anything they tell you is confidential, but we have to
check Mr. Boggs' story. It's important."

"Yes, Judy? What about it?" asked her father.

"You tell him, Peter," Judy suggested. "You're the
one who thinks John Dent may be dead."

"Dead!" exclaimed Horace. "There's been no news
of his death in the papers."

"There wouldn't be," Judy explained, "if Mr. Boggs
decided to keep it a secret."

"But why would he want to do that?"

"It's just a theory of mine," Peter explained. "I
haven't any facts to back it up. He must have some
reason for keeping people away from the castle, and
that might be it. What do you think, sir?"

"He said he called on you to renew a prescription

for him, Dad," Judy put in. "He told us John Dent was a cripple and that you were his doctor—"

"John Dent," Dr. Bolton repeated thoughtfully. "I've heard of him, of course. There are plenty of stories about his strange life in that ruined old castle. But I don't remember ever having seen the man. I was never called to the castle. Never set foot inside it, and certainly I did not renew any prescription for him this morning. Mr. Boggs came to me because of insomnia. He wanted sleeping pills, but I gave him a tonic. Actually, I could find nothing organically wrong with the man."

"Then he did lie to us!" exclaimed Judy. "Oh, Peter! If he lied about the medicine he may have lied about the children, too! He could have given us wrong answers to all our questions. And if he did—"

She stopped, alarmed by her thoughts, while Peter explained to Dr. Bolton what children she meant, and acquainted him with a few more facts.

"I think I have the picture," Judy's father said finally. "According to Mr. Boggs, I am John Dent's doctor—and doctors usually do visit their patients. I may pay him a surprise visit one of these days."

"Oh, Dad! I wish you would. There's so much we didn't find out. I'm sure you could help us. Why would that man tell such conflicting stories?"

"He could be manufacturing them on purpose to confuse people."

"But why would he do it, Dad? He must have known we would check with you."

"Obviously, he wanted us to leave before we found out anything," Peter began, "and we fell for it."

"You mean I did. It was my fault," confessed Judy. "I actually ran out on a mystery we might have stayed and solved."

"You'll solve it yet," Dr. Bolton predicted. "Be careful, though. You may run into trouble."

"I know," Judy said. "I think Mr. Boggs doesn't want the mystery solved, really. He wants people to think the castle is haunted and that John Dent sits up there all day counting his money—"

She broke off at a warning glance from Peter. Horace failed to notice it, but Dr. Bolton did. She had been about to mention the gold piece they had found and ask if it could possibly be part of the lost purchase money that John Dent was supposed to have.

"I mean," she said, "how do we know Mr. Boggs hasn't cheated John Dent out of everything? He may not be crippled, either, the way Mr. Boggs says. He may be dead!"

"I can check the county statistics and maybe see a few people about some other things if I get to the courthouse fast. The offices close at five o'clock and it's nearly that, now. Want to come with me, Judy?" asked Peter.

Judy did want to come. It was only a short drive to

the courthouse, as Farringdon was the county seat for both Roulsville and Farringdon. The castle was in a remote wooded section of the county.

"A hundred years ago people around here went sort of castle-happy, I guess," Judy remarked as they drove past the Farringdon-Pett mansion.

Peter grinned his appreciation of Judy's comment. Two of Judy's dearest friends lived in the mansion, and at one time she had been just a little envious of them. Once she had wanted Lois Farringdon-Pett for her best friend although she knew that Lois and Lorraine Lee were like cup and saucer.

The "house with turrets like a castle" where they both lived still held a sort of fairy-tale enchantment for Judy. She and Peter had been married on the spacious lawn. It had been a double wedding ceremony. Lorraine had married Arthur Farringdon-Pett at the same time. Judy caught sight of the two chums just leaving the house, and hailed them.

"Why walk when you can ride downtown in the Beetle?" she asked them. "Like it?"

Lois and Lorraine were enthusiastic over the new car. They had to laugh when they saw Blackberry still asleep next to the rear window.

"He's worn out," Peter explained. "He spent the morning exploring a castle—"

"Not Lars Olsen's? I've heard of it," Lois said. "It was built about the time our ancestors first settled

Farringdon and built this turreted monstrosity—"

"Lois!" Lorraine exclaimed, shocked.

"Well, it is and you know it," Lois retorted as they drove away from it.

"But, Lois," Lorraine said, "it used to be all the style to have turrets and stone lions and little recessed places for statues—"

"To scare people," giggled Lois. "By the way, is this castle furnished?"

"I wish I knew," replied Judy with a shiver.

"There's a lot we wish we knew," Peter said.

"Maybe there are ghosts in it! What fun!" cried Lois. "Can we help you explore the castle?"

"Arthur and I saw the 'No Trespassing' signs one day when we drove past, and we didn't think anyone was allowed to explore it," Lorraine put in.

"We weren't allowed," Judy said. "Blackberry was the only one who did any real exploring, and he can't tell us what he saw inside the castle walls. We did hear ghostly violin music."

"You did!"

"Yes, and Mr. Boggs couldn't explain it except with some weird story about Lars Olsen coming back to play his violin."

"Careful!" Peter warned. At first Judy couldn't tell whether or not he was serious. "You're helping spread the rumor that the castle is haunted, and that appears to be exactly what Mr. Boggs wants."

"Who is Mr. Boggs?" asked Lois.

"The castle caretaker," replied Judy. "We expect to find out more about him very soon, don't we, Peter?"

"You bet we do!"

He explained his errand at the courthouse in a few words and suggested that the girls stop in the Yellow Bowl and have sodas while they were waiting for him.

"Here comes Honey," he added as he saw his sister approaching, "just in time to join you and help you plan the next thing to do."

CHAPTER XI

Plans and Possibilities

PETER's sister had just come out of the office of the Dean Studios where she worked as an artist. She was hurried off to the Yellow Bowl while everybody talked at once, trying to tell her about the castle.

"It must have been frustrating," she said when she had heard the story, "to be so near the famous castle and not be able to explore it."

"And you know how Judy loves to explore things," Lois and Lorraine chimed in.

"Cup and saucer harmony. You still do it," Honey said with a laugh, "just the way you did when we were in high school together."

"Why not? Being sisters-in-law is even better than being best friends," Lois confided.

Judy squeezed Honey's hand under the table.

"We know," they said to each other.

Suddenly Judy wanted to include them all in her plans. She told them about Granny Joerg, and they found it hard to believe that the daughter of the man who had built the castle was still living.

"Let's go to the old lady's birthday party together," Judy suggested impulsively.

"Could we?"

Suddenly Lois and Lorraine were full of plans.

"We could bring a cake with a hundred candles on it, and party favors and—"

"How could she blow out so many?" asked Honey.

"She'll need them for light," declared Judy. "I'm sure there isn't any electricity in the castle. The Joergs don't have it. You'll be stepping back in time—"

"And loving it!" Lois interrupted.

She whispered something to Lorraine. It seemed to be a delightful secret. Judy hated to spoil their pleasure in planning the birthday party, but she felt she ought to warn them that it might not be held in the castle.

"There's something very mysterious going on there," she finished. "Before we do any more planning, I think we ought to find out what it is."

"How?" her friends questioned all at once. "May we help you?"

"We could sort of invade the castle in force," giggled Honey.

"The children were planning something like that," Judy remembered.

And then she had to tell them about the twins and how Mr. Boggs had lied to them about so many things that she feared he might have been lying when he said he had chased the children home.

"In other words," Lois said, "he's a great big *rail*."

At that Lorraine forgot herself and laughed so hard she nearly choked on her soda. After a few moments, Judy joined in the laughter. Honey looked bewildered.

"What's so funny about the word *rail?*"

"Spell it backwards," Judy suggested.

"It's a secret language Lorraine and I used to have," Lois explained when she managed to stop laughing. "There were certain words we weren't supposed to use. They weren't ladylike, and so we turned them around and used them anyway. Try it sometime."

"Seriously, though," Honey said, "I do think, Judy, you ought to find out for sure about the children. Can't you telephone or something?"

"They don't have a phone and I don't believe any of the neighbors do, either. They live exactly the way people did a hundred years ago. There's even a sign on one of the barns to ward away witches—"

"Witches!" exclaimed Lois. "Oh, Judy! How exciting! Does Granny Joerg look anything like a witch? I should think she'd have a million wrinkles if she's that old. How does she look?"

"You'll see when we go to her party. If Horace is well enough—"

"Wait a minute!" Honey interrupted. "You didn't tell us Horace was sick."

"Didn't I? I thought I had."

Honey was all concern. She wanted to go back to the house with Judy and find out how he was.

"Maybe there's something I can do. It's funny, but I just can't imagine Horace sick. He's always so full of pep and the first to be on hand when anything is going on. I really adore that brother of yours, Judy!"

Judy laughed.

"Enough to give up seeing Forrest Dean?"

Forrest Dean was the handsome son of Honey's employer. She had been seeing a lot of him lately.

"Well," Honey began, and then looked at Judy with a quizzical expression that made Lois and Lorraine laugh, too. "Just how sick *is* Horace?"

"He was feeling like 'a wrung-out dishrag' this morning. I'm quoting," explained Judy, "so I don't have to say it backwards. You didn't know it, Honey, because you weren't around then, but Horace used to be sick a lot when he was a boy. I think I was actually a little jealous of the attention he was always getting, but not any more. Right now, it seems to me he could stand a little attention, especially from you."

Honey had no answer for that. The girls were still teasing her about her rival suitors when Peter came in.

"Ready, Judy?" he inquired. "We'd better get back to the car. Blackberry is shut inside," he added, "and cats don't like confinement."

"Neither do people," Lorraine spoke up. "That's why I can't understand John Dent living all by himself in a ruined castle and hiring a caretaker to chase people away. I should think he'd die of loneliness. I would."

"If he's dead," Peter said grimly, "he didn't die of loneliness. There's no record of his death in the county files, but that doesn't necessarily mean he's still living. As for the Joerg twins—"

"If anything's happened to them," declared Judy, "I'll never forgive myself. Never! Peter didn't want to come back so soon," she explained to her friends. "It was my idea, and now I think we ought to drive back there."

"Tonight?"

Judy nodded.

"It may be a little spooky after dark," Lorraine suggested.

"It was spooky in the daytime," declared Judy. "It will be positively chilling at night."

"*And* thrilling! We'd love to go with you," Lois suddenly exclaimed. "Could we?"

"Do all three of you want to go?" Judy asked in surprise.

They assured her that they did. First, of course,

they'd stop and see Horace. After that they didn't see any reason why they shouldn't all go along for the ride.

"Shall we take them, Peter?" Judy questioned.

"Why not?" said Peter. "It'll be simply a matter of stopping in and asking Mrs. Joerg if the twins got home safely—"

"And of course they did," Judy said uneasily.

"Of course," everybody agreed.

CHAPTER XII

The Man from Mars

NOTHING was said either then or later to make the proposed trip to the ruined castle seem anything more than a pleasant drive out into the country. The girls telephoned home that they would be late, and then went to see Horace before starting off. It was not what they said, but what they didn't say, that made him suddenly suspicious. "Just what sort of a crazy plot are you girls hatching?" he demanded.

"Nothing, Horace. Nothing at all," they told him.

"As soon as Peter's through telephoning, or whatever he's doing in Dad's office," Judy said, "we really have to go. Horace," she added, "do you mind if I leave Blackberry with you? He might be a nuisance."

"A nuisance!" Horace exclaimed. "Why, that cat's

a blessing wherever you take him. You know how many times he's helped you with clues and things. I'll look after him if you insist, but I'll have to shut him up somewhere. He and my parrot don't agree."

"Then we'll borrow your parrot," Judy suddenly decided. "Does he still call names whenever anyone passes his cage?"

"He does unless his cage is covered or it's very dark."

"It's apt to be very, very dark around the castle by the time we get there," Honey said.

"You'll just drive by it? You won't go in?"

"Not unless we're invited," Judy said mysteriously. She gave the parrot a few instructions which sent Lois and Lorraine off into gales of laughter.

"That bird doesn't have to say 'Rail' backwards," they told each other. "He says it right out."

"He'll be perfect for our purpose," declared Judy. "We'll plant him where Mr. Boggs can hear him as soon as the sun comes up tomorrow morning. Then, if he did lie—"

"I get it," grinned Horace. "The parrot will accuse him of it. Boy! Would I like to be there to watch the fun. Can't someone else play nursemaid to your cat?"

"Now, Horace," Judy said, "you want to be well in time for the birthday party, don't you? Well, if you do, you'll take it easy until then."

"And mind your cat. I get it. Well, I wish you luck

invading the castle in case the twins haven't returned. That is what you're afraid of, isn't it?"

"Horace, I don't know. We're driving back there to find out—"

"And you're afraid to take your cat but perfectly willing that your friends should go along?"

"There's safety in numbers," Judy said. "Besides, Blackberry might cause a disturbance."

"And so you're taking the parrot who is sure to? I give up. I guess I just don't understand women," Horace concluded with a sigh, as he walked with the girls to the front door. Judy could not resist a parting dig.

"You sure didn't understand old Granny Joerg," she laughed.

"I can hardly wait to meet her. Come on, Judy," urged Lois. "Peter's ready to start and we may get there before dark if we hurry. Isn't that your father with him?"

Dr. Bolton's back was turned. He and Peter were engaged in what seemed to be a serious conversation out by the car.

"Oh, no! That means Dad objects to the trip. I'll make him change his mind," resolved Judy as she flew down the walk to get her cat.

"Isn't anyone staying for supper?" Mrs. Bolton called anxiously from the door.

"Blackberry is," Judy laughed, returning with the

cat in her arms. "Take him, Mom! Horace has promised to look after him. Would you save something for the rest of us? We'll be famished by the time we get back. It may be late, so don't wait up for us, and don't worry if we're not there in the morning. We may decide to drive back to Dry Brook Hollow."

Judy gave her mother a hug and ran down the path to where the others stood waiting.

"I do object," Dr. Bolton was saying as her friends looked at him in disbelief. "It may be extremely dangerous to enter the castle—"

"We won't enter it, Dad," Judy said. "We'll just drive by it on the way to the Joergs' and maybe stop off long enough to show the girls what we found behind a stone in the castle wall."

"Did you find something, Judy? Do let's hurry up before it gets too dark to see," Honey urged the others.

"We'll just put this in the back of the car," Lois said innocently as she and Lorraine secreted the parrot, cage and all, in the luggage compartment.

"Cheat!" the bird remarked as the door closed upon him.

"What was that?" Dr. Bolton asked, startled.

Judy was laughing so hard that she could not answer. She climbed in beside Peter, who suspected what the girls were up to, and they all rode off in high spirits.

"I guess your father knows you have Horace's parrot back there and has a pretty good idea what you intend to do with him," Peter said when they were well out into the country.

"And what do you intend to do with him?" Honey asked.

Judy outlined her plan and the girls in the back seat enlarged upon it.

"Then," Judy concluded, "when morning comes and light descends on the parrot's cage he will begin to call names from his hiding place. And so when Dad comes to see his patient—"

"What patient?" asked Peter.

"John Dent," Judy explained. "Mr. Boggs himself said he was Dad's patient and so he can't refuse Dad admittance to the castle. By that time, Mr. Boggs will be so tired of hearing the parrot—"

"And of course he won't know it's only a parrot," Lois interrupted. "Those echoes you told us about will pick up its voice and make it sound hollow. That will give him a real scare."

"He'll think a voice from nowhere is accusing him," Lorraine added.

"Some supernatural neighbor," Honey giggled.

"Anyway," Judy finished, "my theory is that he will become so tired of hearing himself called a cheat and a liar that he will break down and tell the truth."

Everybody agreed that this plan sounded promising,

although Peter did say he approved of Judy's motives more than he did of her methods. The giggling subsided after that, and what little talk there was concerned the changing scenery along the turnpike.

There was something different about it. Judy was puzzled at first. Then she decided the change was brought about by the storm which had blown the autumn leaves off the trees, leaving them bare.

The air became almost oppressive as they approached the castle. Soon they could see it on the hilltop, its turrets like giant fingers reaching toward the dusky sky. The sun had set, leaving a weird brightness in the west. Below the castle, the forest was already dark.

"I didn't think it would be this far from the road," Lois said as Peter stopped the car and they all hopped out. "How do we get up there?"

"There's a path," he began, but Judy had already found it.

"Can we see our way?" Lorraine asked, beginning to get an attack of the shivers.

"I think so," Judy said. "If not, I have my flash."

"We won't go in?"

"We can't, silly! We'll just leave the parrot outside the wall, the way we planned. Peter is bringing it."

Stopping for the cage had slowed him up a little. It was Judy who led the way past the waterfall she remembered. The path seemed different, somehow. Judy had forgotten that it went through a pine woods where the trees stood close together, and then up a steep incline. It was very dark in the shadow of the castle wall.

"In a minute, I'm going to show you the initials," Judy called to her friends, who were following.

Lois and Lorraine stopped as a sound was heard of someone breaking through the brush.

"Look! Look!" screamed Honey.

Turning, she rushed headlong down the path with Lois and Lorraine close behind her. They nearly bumped into Peter, who was just climbing up with the cage in his hand.

"It's coming after us!" they cried breathlessly, too frightened to say more.

"Judy!" Peter shouted so loudly that the castle walls sent back an echo.

"I'm all right," she answered. "I'm coming."

She could not imagine what had frightened everybody so until she looked back. Then she saw it! She stood absolutely still for a moment, unable to believe the evidence of her own eyes.

"It's a man from Mars!" she gasped. "It must be."

Watching in horrified fascination, she saw a plumed figure that could not possibly be human stride right through the castle wall.

CHAPTER XIII

"Not Again!"

"Judy!" Peter called for a second time.

"I'll b-be with you in a minute," she replied shakily. "I—I dropped my flashlight."

She did not say she had dropped it after she had flashed it full upon the apparition. Light from what looked like a glittering metallic body had flashed back at her with such shocking suddenness that she simply dropped the light and stood frozen.

After her first moment of panic, Judy was seized with a desire to see the whole of the figure she had merely glimpsed. She tried to tell herself that its metallic body might be nothing more than a shining kettle lid someone had carelessly tossed in a tree. But there

84

were arms and legs! Could they have been merely tree shadows? Had she really seen waving plumes on the figure's head or were they only the ferns she now observed growing out of the castle wall? She couldn't find the carved initials or the loose stone without her flashlight. She wasn't even sure she had taken the right path.

"I'll have to find my way back," she thought, groping around among the dry leaves at her feet.

In another moment Peter was with her.

"What happened, Angel?" he asked, taking her in his arms and kissing her tenderly. "Judy girl, you're trembling. Here's your flashlight. It must have rolled down the path when you dropped it. Shall we go back to the car?"

"I—I guess so," she faltered. "What about the p-parrot?"

Judy couldn't help stuttering. Her teeth were still chattering from fright.

"Honey took it back to the car. We'll forget all that nonsense and find out what really happened. Isn't that what you want to do?"

"I—I guess so, Peter. I thought I saw—I don't know what."

"The girls were babbling something about an invasion by the Martians," he said. "To hear them talk you'd think they saw a whole horde of iron men."

"No, there was only one. Sort of a birdlike figure

with plumes on his head. His body was made of some metal that flashed back the light when I tried to see him. It really was frightening. Where are the girls now?"

"In the car, I hope. Can you walk a little faster? We ought not to leave them alone."

Judy agreed. Holding tightly to Peter's hand, she followed as fast as she could.

"Peter, I just thought of something," she said as he hurried along. "It could have been a figure in armor."

"Mr. Boggs, probably, rigged up on purpose to scare people away from the castle," Peter declared. "And we were going to scare *him!*"

Judy was laughing at her fears by the time she and Peter reached the car. The girls were huddled inside. No amount of explaining could calm their terror.

"Did you really see it go through the wall?" Lois asked. "There isn't any opening, is there?"

"No, only one loose stone. It had initials on it," Judy said. "That's what I was going to show you."

"You didn't plan this, did you, Judy?" Honey asked suspiciously.

"Why would Judy plan to scare herself?" asked Lois. "She was just as frightened as we were. It *had* to be something supernatural to go right through a wall," she added solemnly.

Judy's thoughts flashed back to other mysteries that had puzzled her—the apparent ghosts, the voices, the portrait that had seemed to be alive, even the transparent figure she had once seen walking in her garden. How many times had she thought, "It has to be something supernatural," only to find out later that there was always an explanation. Once she started using her head, as her father so often advised her, she was no longer frightened—just curious.

"There was a door in the wall," she said now. "Peter and I saw what looked like a door panel behind that loose stone I meant to show you. Maybe Mr. Boggs has some way of opening the walled-in door and jumping out to scare people."

"It's an idea," Peter agreed. "Those stones were pretty solid, though."

"Could they have been removed?" asked Lois, suddenly so interested she didn't want to leave. "That would be a way into the castle, wouldn't it?"

"A secret way," Honey whispered. "Imagine! And we were so near."

"Shall we go back?"

It was Judy who asked this question.

"We ought to make sure the twins are safe before we take on anything else," declared Peter.

"I should have investigated," Judy said. "If only I hadn't been so frightened—"

"Of course, whoever planned it knew you would be," Honey put in wisely.

Lois giggled.

"And hoped you'd think the castle was haunted."

"I'll bet something precious that's just what Mr. Boggs intended me to think, if it was he who rigged himself up like that," declared Judy.

"It didn't look human," Honey said, still mystified.

"Maybe—maybe it wasn't," Lorraine faltered, finding her voice. The creature had given her a real scare. She was still trembling.

Judy giggled. "I thought it was a man from Mars with an invisible ray gun or something."

"When all the time it probably was old man Boggs dressed up in a tin overcoat," Peter finished.

They made it sound so ridiculous that even Lorraine finally was convinced it had been a trick played on them by the castle caretaker.

"Something like our parrot trick," Lois concluded, "only his trick worked."

"A man like that wouldn't have been frightened by a parrot anyway," Judy began. "He might have killed it."

She told the girls now how Mr. Boggs had tried to steal the leopard coat she was wearing.

"He meant to take it, too," she declared. "He lied when he said he only intended to find out who had left it there."

"Where?" Honey asked.

The story she had heard, bit by bit from Judy and Peter, was confusing.

"On a bush," Judy explained. "I left it there when I climbed the tree that leans over the castle wall. I wanted to see what was going on in the castle."

"And did you?"

"Not a thing. It looked quite deserted except for a few chickens and that blue car parked inside the wall. How Mr. Boggs drove it in there, I really can't imagine. We couldn't find any road to the castle, only a lot of confusing paths."

"That's queer."

"It certainly is," agreed Judy. "It gets queerer and queerer the more I think of it. That man has something to hide. I'm sure of it."

"I hope you aren't thinking what I'm thinking. If you are, we'd better get out of here—and fast," Peter said, starting the car.

"I can guess what you're thinking," Judy told him, "but the way I have it figured out, it isn't a body. Who plays the violin if John Dent is dead? Surely not our man from Mars."

"Let's not talk about him any more," Lorraine protested with a shiver. "I still can't believe I saw what I thought I saw. We should have driven on past the castle and stopped at the Joerg house to inquire about the children first. Aren't we nearly there?"

"As soon as we round the next curve," Peter began, but stopped abruptly to jam on the brakes.

Everyone was tense from the experience of a few

moments before. The girls in the back seat screamed, and Lorraine nearly fainted.

"Oh, Peter! Not again!" Judy cried out in dismay as she glimpsed a dark figure in the road and then watched it vanish almost before her eyes.

CHAPTER XIV

Still Missing

"THAT was close!" Peter exclaimed as the car screeched to a stop. "I didn't expect anybody to be walking beside the road along here. Are you girls all right?"

"Only scared half to death, that's all," Lois gasped. "Lorraine's as white as a sheet. Did you see who it was in the road?"

Lorraine murmured something that was more like a gulp than a sentence.

"Who could see her?" Honey wanted to know. "She had something over her head."

"Like an old witch," whispered Lois. "She was all in black."

"On her way to help His Majesty from Mars haunt

the castle, no doubt. But what happened to her?"
asked Judy.

"I caught a glimpse of her," Peter said, and he was
serious. "She darted or fell into the bushes at the side
of the road. I hope I didn't hit her."

"Oh, Peter! I'm sorry. I shouldn't have joked about
it," Judy apologized. "I'll help you find her."

She jumped out of the car with Peter, who examined
the road first and then began searching through the
brush at the side of it. There was no indication of anyone having been hit.

Honey followed to help them search. Lois stayed
in the back seat of the car with Lorraine's head in her
lap. Judy took one look at them and thought to herself, "Lorraine can be so beautifully helpless."

"Peter," she said impulsively, "why don't I ever
faint and let you hold my head and comfort me? Don't
you wish I would?"

"I don't ever wish you any different than you are,"
he said, and Judy knew he meant it. "I wouldn't
change a hair on your silly red head, even for the sake
of holding it. Now are you satisfied?"

"I wouldn't change you, either," Judy replied in a
sudden rush of tenderness.

He grinned in the boyish way she loved.

"Well, now that we've settled that, let's see if we
can't find out what happened here. There was a
woman walking beside the road and I'm pretty sure

I didn't hit her. But I don't see her now. Honey!" he called to his sister. "Did you see what happened to her?"

"No doubt she vanished," Honey replied from behind the car where she was searching through the things in the luggage compartment for the flashlight. "Did you notice the way she walked?"

"It was sort of mechanical," Judy admitted, "but she might simply be old and stiff."

"She certainly might," agreed Peter. "Now you're using your head, Angel."

"I thought she looked a little like—"

"Listen!" Peter interrupted, raising a finger.

What they heard was something between a laugh and a cackle. Judy still could not see her, but she immediately recognized the cracked old voice.

It was Granny Joerg!

"Scare a body to death, will you?" she muttered as she emerged from the bushes, walking stiffly with the aid of her cane. Peter offered to assist her, but she refused, saying, "I can still help myself. As if I didn't have enough trouble without you practically running me down!" She whirled on Judy and demanded, "What did you do with my children?"

Now Judy could see her, a pathetic figure in her long black dress. The shawl over her head did make her look like a witch. But it was Judy she accused of witchcraft. Her jumbled muttering ended with a repetition of the question, "What did you do with my children?"

"Nothing, Mrs. Joerg," Judy answered. "We haven't—"

"Hiram Boggs said you came here to stir up trouble," Granny Joerg broke in. "He said—"

"Liar!" shrieked a raucous voice from the back of the car.

Poor Granny jumped and clutched at Judy.

"It's only a parrot," Peter explained.

"I didn't mean to wake him up," apologized Honey, who had just found the flashlight and turned it on. "I had forgotten he was in the luggage compartment. Light does strange things to him."

"He's right, though. Mr. Boggs did lie," Judy said. "We were going to plant the parrot in the castle—"

"The way you took the children?"

"But we didn't," Judy protested. "We were coming back to ask you about them. Did they get home safely?"

"You know they didn't!" shrieked the nearly hysterical old lady. "They haven't come home at all!"

Judy and Peter looked at each other in dismay. Their worst fears were confirmed. The twins were still missing and they were being blamed for it.

"I was warned that you two were up to no good," Granny raved on. "It's a curse on me that I must live to see the last of my children die. I was warned—"

"That we had put such a curse on you?" Judy gasped.

"Who warned you?" demanded Peter.

Judy was not surprised to hear that it was Hiram Boggs, the castle caretaker.

"He said the last he saw of the children was when you whisked them into your car and drove off with them. He said he tried to stop you," Granny finished.

"And you believed him? But of course you would," Judy said more thoughtfully. "I'm surprised that he said it was a car and not a broom, but I suppose he had to make his fairy story believable. I believed him, too. But you were suspicious of him all along, weren't you, Peter?"

"Only a little," he admitted. "Obviously, these conflicting stories were meant to confuse us and keep us from finding out what really happened to the children. Mr. Boggs told us he saw them running down the road toward home just a few minutes after we'd left to look for them. Naturally, we assumed they were safe—"

Suddenly Granny's thin frame was wracked by sobs. She cried out that they were not safe and that she had to get them back. She began screaming more accusations, but Peter stopped her. Judy knew his voice could be kind, but now it was firm as well.

"You must listen to us, Mrs. Joerg," he told her. "We want to help you. We'll search the castle tonight if necessary. This time Boggs will have to let us in."

"He won't do it!" she cried. "I've just come from there and he wouldn't open the gate for me. He declared up and down he'd seen you steal the children. I'll find out if he lied to me! I'll get the law on him!"

"Good for you!" applauded Honey, beginning to clap her hands.

Lois and Lorraine poked inquisitive heads out of the car window and quickly drew them back at the sight of Granny still screaming that she'd get the police or the FBI.

Judy and Peter exchanged significant glances.

"You have the FBI here right now, Mrs. Joerg," Judy finally managed to tell her. "Peter, show her your credentials."

Under the flashlight which Honey held in a somewhat unsteady hand, Granny was able to read enough of what was on Peter's identification card to convince her that Judy was telling the truth. But still she fumed.

"Why didn't you say so this afternoon? Why didn't you tell me the children were in danger?"

"I wish we had known it," Peter replied in a voice that anyone could tell was sincere. Judy loved the way he suddenly made everything as plain as day simply by explaining, step by step, what had actually taken place.

"You see," he finished, "the children were curious about all this, too. They did slide down a tree branch inside the castle wall. We're pretty sure of that. But Mr. Boggs said he'd chased them home. His story

sounded so convincing that, unfortunately, we believed him."

"You mean I did," Judy said ruefully. "It wasn't
until after we questioned my father that we began to
suspect Mr. Boggs had lied to us about everything."

"And then we thought of the parrot," Honey
added. "We were going to take it along and hide it
somewhere near the castle to frighten him. We never
meant it to frighten you."

"Just the caretaker, eh?" Granny actually chuckled
as she began to understand. But she was quite serious a
moment later when she turned to Peter and inquired,
"Do you carry a gun with you, young man?"

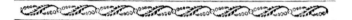

CHAPTER XV

The Hidden Road

THE question surprised Judy more than it did Peter. He assured Granny Joerg that he was armed and that he had authority to investigate anything suspicious at the castle.

"Then what are we waiting for?" she asked. "I'm willing to ride back there with you and show the old skinflint we mean business. You can still plant your talking bird to scare him into telling the truth and I'll help you."

"Think you ought to chance it?" asked Peter. "We may run into danger."

"Nothing you can't handle, I'm sure," Judy told him confidently. "We will all be right behind you."

Still Peter hesitated.

"What about the police?" he asked. "Has anyone

notified them, Mrs. Joerg, about the missing children?"

"My great-grandson will tell them. He said he would if they weren't home by eight o'clock, and it's past eight now."

Granny was growing impatient. Judy couldn't help admiring her spirit. It seemed little hampered by her frail old body as she hobbled over toward the car. What an adventurous soul she must have been when she was young!

"Like those precious twins," thought Judy, and suddenly she was seized with a fierce determination to find them at all costs. Her heart went out to poor Granny, who was so afraid she would live to see them die. "It mustn't happen," Judy resolved, "and it won't if I can help it. Only a fiend would put such a fear in an old lady's mind."

Peter must have guessed her thoughts. He surprised her by giving her a quick kiss and whispering in her ear, "I'm determined to find them, too."

Honey, who was used to helping old people, was walking with Granny. She introduced Lois and Lorraine, who were so polite that they won her over completely. Soon they were all on their way back to the castle.

"We'll show him," Granny was muttering. "He can't lock up my darlings and get away with it. He's put them in the dungeon and the good Lord only knows what he's done with poor John Dent."

"Does the castle have a dungeon?" Judy ventured.

"Most folks don't think so," she answered vaguely.

"But you know it has?" Peter prompted her.

Granny was now seated comfortably beside Honey in the back seat of the car. Lois and Lorraine had moved over to make room for her. She nodded vigorously.

"I know there used to be a dungeon. My father had it built for reasons of his own."

"What reasons?" ventured Honey.

Granny said she didn't know what reasons, but she felt sure they were good ones.

Judy couldn't think of any good reason for building a dungeon, but decided not to say so. Instead, she asked, "Did Mr. Boggs know about it?"

"Nobody knows what he knew or what he's up to," declared Granny. "That's what I told my great-grandson before I set out for the castle. I said like as not he'd locked the twins up because they were getting too curious. But he said more likely they'd gone exploring and got themselves lost in the woods. He's out searching for them now and some of the neighbors are helping, though I wouldn't trust them."

"I can understand that," said Peter.

He was so interested that he would have missed the main road up to the castle if Granny hadn't pointed it out.

"The twins told me about it. They're onto his tricks. See that fallen hemlock tree? Looks like a row of little scrub hemlocks unless you examine it closely."

"Yes? What about it?" asked Peter, stopping the car.

"It hides the road. You can move it to one side and drive right on up the hill."

Peter gave a low whistle of surprise.

"A whole tree?" asked Judy.

The girls in the back seat echoed her amazement. It did not take Peter long to discover how it worked, though. A pulley and ropes were conveniently attached so that the little hemlock could be raised or lowered at will without disturbing the roots of the tree enough to make it wither.

This time the tree was raised but not lowered. With Judy's help, Peter secured the ropes to another tree so that the hemlock remained standing in an upright position.

"The ropes show," Judy commented as the moon came out from behind a cloud and gave the white ropes a ghostly appearance.

"I hoped they would," Peter replied.

Judy did not understand what he meant at first. But he soon explained it.

"We'll leave the road clear just in case someone follows us," he said when he was once more at the wheel

and the car was on its way up the narrow little road
that had appeared, as if by magic, when the tree was
raised.

"The police?" Granny questioned.

"Yes, or anyone else who wants to investigate the
queer goings on at the castle. Now I know it must be
some sort of a hideout. Why else would it have a con-
cealed entrance? A truck has been driven up here
recently, too."

Peter made this observation as they climbed the next
steep curve.

"How recently?" asked Judy.

"Within the past week or so, but I'd have to check
the tire prints before I could be sure," he replied.

"It gets more and more puzzling, doesn't it?" asked
Honey.

"Yes, and darker and darker," agreed Lois with a
shiver. "The moon keeps popping in and out from behind those clouds. I'm not sure I like it."

"Me, either," chattered Lorraine. "It's cold, too."

"The castle does have sort of a chill around it," admitted Judy. "But you can see the entrance now.
Look, the moon is out again and everything has put on
a glow."

It was true. The sudden moonlight had spread a sil-
very whiteness over the whole castle, making it look
like a picture out of a book of fairy tales. Trees, fallen
rocks, and other objects appeared to be in full daylight

except for their darker shadows. What a night it was for just such an adventure as this one promised to be!

At the great arched entrance Peter stopped the car. An iron gate barred the way. It looked as if it were meant to be raised or perhaps let down to form a ramp. The castle actually had a little moat around it. Here it was quite deep and filled with water. Below the wall, Judy remembered, it had been little more than a ditch with no water in it at all.

"This must be the head of that rippling stream that forms the waterfall we saw, Peter," she said thoughtfully. "Maybe it flows underground, like Dry Brook back home."

"That's something else to puzzle about," he agreed. "This is as far as we go, folks! Everybody out! It looks safe enough."

"It looks beautiful," breathed Honey when they were all out of the car and standing beside the moat where the moonlight made dancing reflections in the water. "What a shame Horace had to be ill and miss this!"

"It is a shame, isn't it?" agreed Lois. "Peter, do you think we'll really be admitted to the castle?"

"One way or another," he replied mysteriously.

"Are you thinking of trying the secret entrance?" Judy whispered excitedly. "The way that—that man from Mars went in? I mean, if we aren't admitted through the front gate?"

"I think I understand what you mean," Peter replied with a chuckle. "We'll think about it after we've tried the obvious way into the castle."

"But we can't get over there," Lois protested. "How can we ring the bell, if there is a bell?"

"You can holler," Granny Joerg said suddenly. "If you holler loud enough it'll bring somebody out. You mark my words."

"Shall we?" asked Judy dubiously.

She wasn't at all eager to stir up the echoes again, and everyone else agreed with her. Then Honey thought of the parrot.

"We could find a log and push it across the moat and carry the cage over and hide it the way we planned. Let's do it," she suggested.

"Wait!" Judy told her. "See that flickering light down there? Two men are coming up the road carrying a lantern. Let's wait and see what they want before we do anything."

CHAPTER XVI

Across the Moat

The two men turned out to be Emil Joerg, the old lady's great-grandson and father of the missing twins, and a neighbor he introduced as Jim Stroup. Granny introduced Peter, who presented Judy and her friends and explained their plans.

"Sounds fine if it works," the twins' father approved. "We didn't have any luck searching the woods, so we thought we'd try the castle. How'd you get here, Granny?"

"Walked," she said. "That is, the first time. I talked with the caretaker. This bird will tell him what I think of what he told me."

"A parrot, eh? Let's hear him talk."

"Ta-alk!" the bird mimicked, sidling along his perch.

"He isn't usually so polite," giggled Honey.

"We hope he won't be when he meets Hiram Boggs," Judy told the two newcomers. "We suspect Boggs knows where the twins are and we're going to make him tell."

"He'd better," muttered Emil Joerg.

He and Jim Stroup offered to help, although Granny glared suspiciously at the latter and mumbled something about not trusting neighbors.

Judy trusted both of them. They appeared to be honest, hard-working farmers and good friends. It did not take them long to find a log that would reach across the moat. But it took the combined strength of all of them to move it.

Meanwhile not a sound nor a flicker of light came from the castle. It looked completely deserted.

"Maybe everybody inside it has been sleeping for a hundred years," Lois suggested, "like someone in a fairy tale."

"Mr. Boggs is the ogre, I guess," Lorraine said.

She was beginning to enjoy the moonlight adventure a little, although not for anything would she have ventured across the log which was now safely in place. Judy was eager to try it. Peter came next, helping Honey, who refused to let him take the birdcage.

"It helps me keep my balance. Whoops!" she exclaimed. "There! I would have fallen if it hadn't been for Horace's parrot. Does it have a name?"

"Horatius, isn't it?" asked Peter.

Judy giggled and would have lost her footing if Peter hadn't steadied her.

"Horatius is right. And is he ever at the bridge! 'Thrice thirty thousand foes before and the broad flood behind.' There, I made it!" she exclaimed, stepping off the log. "Let me take the parrot, Honey! I see just the place to hide him."

Looking up at the crumbling tower at the right of the great arched doorway, Judy had observed a small oblong opening too narrow to be called a window.

"See it?" She pointed. "If you'll boost me up, Peter, I'm sure I can make it. Let me take the flashlight, too. It may be dark inside."

"Maybe you'll find some more gold. Stand on my shoulders and look fast while you're up there," Peter directed as he obligingly lifted Judy, parrot and all, as high as he could.

"What do you see?" Honey asked curiously.

"Nothing much," Judy replied. "It looks like a tool house or something. There's a big chain wound around a post." Her voice was suddenly louder as she exclaimed, "There, it's placed! Now let me down."

The parrot now was peacefully sleeping inside the narrow window on a convenient ledge Judy had found there.

"He won't be so peaceful when daylight hits him," Peter predicted.

"We won't be here then, I hope." Judy was still puzzled. "That chain. I wonder what it's for."

"Maybe to let down the gate," Peter said. "You must have gained a little weight," he added teasingly, as he put Judy down.

"I did it trying to build you up after we found you half starved," she replied, "and now I've let you hurt your arm lifting me. I'm such a blockhead!"

"Objection," Peter said with a grin. "The word is redhead, not blockhead. And you didn't hurt my arm."

"You're sure? Look, Peter!" Judy exclaimed an instant later. She pointed toward the left-hand tower. Like the one on the right, it had been cracked either by lightning or by some other force. It also had a small oblong window that seemed to peer down at her like an eye.

Suddenly she realized that it wasn't the window, but a face inside it that was peering!

"Peter, he's up there," she whispered.

"Mr. Boggs?"

"I think so. He's been up there in the dark watching everything we did. What are we going to do?"

"Exactly what we planned," Peter said. "We'll enter the castle and search for those twins, but now we're going to need help. I'll send one of those men over there for the police just in case we run into trouble."

"Peter, we're sure to," Judy whispered. "Don't try anything too dangerous. I'm afraid for you."

"That's exactly the way I feel," he said, "only it's you I'm afraid for. You and Honey and all the rest—"

"Including the twins. I see," Judy replied.

"I thought you would." Peter turned to the two men, who had crossed the log without Granny in spite of her threats and mutterings. "One of you better go back," he said. "How long will it take you to bring the police? I'm afraid we're going to need help."

"I can get a state trooper here in less than half an hour," Jim Stroup said.

"Do you have a car?"

"Not here. There's one at the farm a couple of miles down the road—"

"Use my car to get there." Peter handed him the keys and scribbled something on a card. "For the police," he explained, showing his own identification. "They'll know it's urgent."

"Get them fast, Jim. I'm going in there with Dobbs and find my kids," declared Emil Joerg.

Across the moat Granny began to moan something about a premonition. She could not cross the log alone and nobody offered to help her.

"What'll we do?" shrieked Lorraine. "You can't go off and leave us standing here. We're afraid to cross."

"I'm not," Lois said, "but I won't cross without you. Both of us could help Mrs. Joerg."

"Don't try it!" Peter warned them.

"But they'll miss all the fun," Honey began, and then stopped at a look from Judy. Two lost children who might be imprisoned in a dungeon weren't fun, her gray eyes said. She dared not think further than that about what might have happened to them, especially if they had found something of value and Mr. Boggs wanted it. But what had they found? Could it have been they who dropped the gold piece Peter had put in his pocket?

Suddenly Judy thought she knew what the twins had found. It came to her in a flash and made her even more fearful for their safety. Had Peter suspected it, too? She wanted to ask him about it. All at once there were a dozen things she wanted to ask him. But now was not the time.

"What's wrong?" Honey whispered, clutching Judy's coat sleeve.

"Nothing—yet," she whispered back.

Peter was waiting on purpose to give Jim Stroup time to go for help, she knew. But Emil Joerg was impatient.

"If he's harmed my kids——" he began. But Peter interrupted with a shout.

"We know you're up there, Mr. Boggs. If you have nothing to conceal, you will open the gate and let us enter peacefully. Two children have been lost and the castle must be searched."

"Impossible," came a voice from the tower. "The master is ill. He must not be disturbed."

"Ill, is he? More likely he's dead," charged Granny Joerg. Her shrill old voice sounded clearly across the moat. "I told you I'd be back if you'd lied to me!"

Honey could not resist the temptation. She turned the flashlight directly on the parrot, who screeched, "Liar!" in a voice that startled everybody, even Judy. Granny was quick to seize the opportunity. She continued to hurl accusations at Hiram Boggs in a voice almost as raucous as the parrot's screech. When she paused for breath, the bird would call the usual forbidden words. Finally Granny hurled the final bombshell.

"Yes, Hiram Boggs, I told you I'd be back. But I didn't tell you I'd have Peter Dobbs with me!"

"And who is Peter Dobbs?" asked the voice from the tower. "Who is he? I know the girl in the leopard coat. She's Dr. Bolton's daughter, calls herself a detective—"

"She should," Granny chuckled. "She's married to Peter Dobbs and he's a G-man! Yes, that's what I said. A G-man, and he's got a gun. You know when to use that gun you're toting, don't you, young fellow?"

"I seldom find it necessary," Peter replied, but his voice was dangerously calm. So was the stillness that followed. Judy knew Peter had not meant Granny to give away his secret so soon, but now it was done and he had to make the best of it.

They waited, hardly daring to breathe, for what would happen next. The silence was broken by the sudden rattle of the chain Judy had seen, as the iron gate began to be lowered—slowly, slowly. Finally it settled itself across the moat and became a bridge. The log Lorraine had been afraid to cross no longer was needed.

"Shall we?" asked Lois.

Seizing Lorraine's hand, she ran across with her. Lorraine protested only mildly, but Judy knew it had taken real courage. Granny hobbled after them with the help of her faithful cane.

"So he's letting us in, is he?" she muttered. "Into a trap, most likely. There he comes with a lantern in his hand and an evil smile on his face. He's up to something, mark my words!"

CHAPTER XVII

Inside the Castle Wall

MR. BOGGS now stood in the great arched entrance to the castle where he peered suspiciously through the iron grillwork of a second gate.

"Better unlock it," Peter directed.

"We'll break it down if you don't. I'll stop at nothing to get those kids of mine out of your hands, Hiram Boggs," declared Emil Joerg.

"There are no children here. You may come in and see for yourselves."

Saying this, Mr. Boggs produced a massive key and obediently unlocked the grilled iron gate. It swung inward at Peter's touch.

"I don't like this," Judy whispered to him. "It's a

little too easy. Mr. Boggs must have a reason we don't suspect for letting us into the castle. Why is he smiling like that?"

"Granny may be right," Peter said. "He may be leading us into a trap. But, if we can trust Jim Stroup, help will soon be on the way."

"But can we?"

"He seemed trustworthy. There is always some risk when you trust a stranger. But, on the other hand," Peter pointed out, "you can't go around being suspicious of everybody. We must all depend on each other to a certain extent and I'm depending on Jim Stroup right now. But let's not be too eager to get inside the castle. We may lose each other. Wait!" Peter called to those who were ahead. "What about searching the ruined towers first?"

Mr. Boggs had been conducting the little company of searchers toward the east tower in the shadow of the castle wall. Now he stepped back into the square of moonlight in the center of the enclosure. The same evil smirk was on his face.

"Just as you like, sir," he assented politely. "I suppose you know, though, that they're condemned and may be dangerous."

"No more dangerous than the trap you may be leading us into," thought Judy.

Peter hesitated, possibly thinking some of the same thoughts that ran through Judy's mind. But, dangerous or not, he was determined to find out what was in the ruined towers.

"The twins may have tried to explore them," he gave as his reason for entering the one that was almost entirely in ruins. The lower part of it had been used as a gatehouse. Mr. Boggs had a cot and chair there, but there was little else except the mechanism that let down the gate. Rubble had fallen from the tower, cutting off the stairs to the top.

"You don't think—" Judy began.

But Peter guessed her thoughts and said, "No, not here. This is what happened when lightning struck it —how long ago?"

"I don't remember," she said, "but it doesn't matter. They aren't here and I'm sure they can't be in the opposite tower where the big chains are."

Peter took a quick look and agreed with her. The parrot, still hidden in the narrow window, didn't make a sound. Honey glanced at him. She was sorely tempted to turn her flashlight on him again, Judy could see, but she was waiting for just the right moment.

"Might as well get a little fun out of this gloomy expedition," she whispered.

"He'll catch you," warned Lois. "The bogeyman is too near. Wait till he moves away a little—"

"Or tells some more of his fairy tales," Lorraine put in.

Judy had an idea.

"What about the far tower?" she asked. "Shall **we** look over there?"

"If you wish," Mr. Boggs replied, turning to walk in that direction. "But you'll disturb the chickens at this hour."

"Chickens!" all three girls exclaimed.

"We saw them," Judy began, but Granny broke in with an ancient cackle.

"He's telling the truth for once," she said. "That tower was never finished, so John put in chicken roosts and boxes for the hens to lay their eggs in. Or was it his father? It must've been," she decided after a moment during which she tapped her cane as she thought it over. "He kept a few geese, too. Maybe that's why I like my old goose so much. Reminds me of one I used to have when I lived here."

"How long ago was that?" asked Lois.

"Ages," she said. "I lose track of time."

She seemed lost in thought for a moment, with time, like a heavy load, on her bent old shoulders. Her cane seemed to be tapping away the minutes of her life as she followed along. Every now and then she would pause to comment sadly on the condition of the grounds.

"Poor Granny!" thought Judy.

And suddenly she was filled with a fierce resolve to make her remaining time on earth as pleasant as possible. Somehow, there had to be a birthday party here where Granny had so many happy memories. But Judy knew there would be no party at all unless the twins were found.

"Shall we look in the far tower and wake up the chickens?" Lois asked. "The twins could have gone in there to play."

"They wouldn't have stayed," Judy began when the caretaker, who had heard the question, broke in with unexpected ferocity.

"Somebody's been going in there to steal eggs," he declared. "I've tried to catch the thief, and when I do—"

"Yes?" Peter prompted him.

The polite Mr. Boggs had dropped his disguise, but only for a moment.

"I would chase him away as I did the twins this afternoon. If it was eggs they came for, they should have brought a basket and I would gladly have given them a few. I told you I sent them home."

"You told Mrs. Joerg a different story," charged Judy. "You made her believe we'd put a curse on her and you told her that the last you'd seen of the twins was when we whisked them into the car and drove away with them."

"Did she tell you that?" asked Mr. Boggs in a surprised tone. "You must realize that her memory is failing. I never said—"

"Liar!" screeched the parrot as Honey walked innocently away from the tower where his cage was secreted.

The caretaker started nervously. "Well, I—it was only to keep Granny from worrying," he admitted weakly.

The old lady gave a snort.

"That's a likely tale. And I'm Mrs. Joerg to you, Hiram Boggs. Only my friends call me Granny."

"May I?" asked Judy.

Now that she knew the truth, Judy hoped the old lady would be more friendly, but it was too soon.

"I'll know who my friends are when the twins are found," she retorted. "I don't trust anybody yet."

"We'll find them if we have to turn this castle upside down," her great-grandson declared. "Where's John Dent?"

The question seemed to startle Mr. Boggs, although he must have expected it.

"In his room," he replied. "Where else could he be? He's a helpless cripple, unable to leave his bed."

"What crippled him?" asked Peter.

"A fall. He broke his leg."

"Who is Mr. Dent's doctor?" demanded Peter.

Judy fully expected the caretaker to tell him once more that it was her father. But this time he said, "He will see no one."

"What's this?" cried Granny. "Who waits on him

then? Who cooks his meals? Have you no housekeeper? Who keeps his room tidy?"

"I do," the caretaker replied. "He sees no one else."

Granny threw up her hands, waving her cane in
violent agitation.

"Poor John!" she cried. "How can you let him stay
up there sick and lonely with nobody to fetch a doctor
or cook him any decent food?"

"I cook for him."

"You?" sneered Granny. "What sort of food could
you cook? It would kill him if he's not dead already!"

"Alive or dead, we mean to find out what's going
on here," declared Emil Joerg. "Where is John Dent?
If my kids got in here they came to see him. Maybe
he knows what happened to them. Where is he, I
say?"

Peter moved toward the caretaker.

"It will be wise, Mr. Boggs," he said, "to answer
that question."

CHAPTER XVIII

Stolen!

THE question was repeated.

"Where is John Dent?"

It was no longer possible for Mr. Boggs to give anything but a direct answer.

"Up there," he said, pointing toward the east tower.

Judy's gray eyes followed the direction of his pointing. She felt a chill go through her as the moon slid behind a cloud, leaving the whole castle in darkness. Honey gave a little gasp and Lois and Lorraine shivered and clung to each other. For a moment nobody said anything. They were all apprehensive, with the possible exception of old Mrs. Joerg and her great-grandson, who seemed beyond all fear in their determination to find the twins.

"If he is up there," Peter said, "I must ask you to show us to his room."

"But, sir," the caretaker protested, "you said you wished to explore the ruined towers—"

He got no further. The expression on Peter's face made it perfectly clear that he was not taking any more excuses.

"Very well, if you insist," Mr. Boggs said, bowing slightly, "I'll lead you to the master's quarters. You will see for yourselves there are no children here. Only the master sits up there in bed or in the chair beside it, propped by his pillows. Day after day I wait on him and serve him. The best of everything goes to the master. You will see for yourselves how well I have cared for him."

"I can see for myself you've let the yard go to wrack and ruin. Where is the garden I remember?" asked Granny as she hobbled along with the others across the enclosure toward the east tower.

She pointed with her cane. "Look there! A hole where John had one of his imported shrubs. There's another! And another!"

Judy was interested. So, apparently, was Peter, although he had nothing to say until they were inside the vast old entrance hall. Then he asked, "Is there any change here, Mrs. Joerg?"

Granny did not answer at once. Her great-grandson, too, surveyed the vaultlike room in silence. So did all the others. They were afraid to make a sound for fear it would split the silence with an echo as Peter's voice had done.

Judy could sense the deep emotion that quieted Granny, for in this very room she must have spent many happy hours. Had she and the Dent girls been like sisters? Surely she had loved John, the youngest, as if he were her own brother. Here she had hoped to celebrate her one hundredth birthday although, in her anxiety, she seemed to have forgotten all about it. Finally she spoke in a hollow whisper.

"There is a change. Now I know poor John is dead and they've kept it from me."

"How do you know?" asked Judy.

Granny's answer was a gesture to indicate the emptiness of the hall that surely had been filled with treasures in former years. There was nothing but one fat candle burning on a long board table to give them light. The table had stone supports apparently cemented to the floor. This was also of stone as were the supports of the few benches that remained to save the room from utter emptiness. Peter pointed out a number of evenly spaced niches along the wall.

"Something has been removed from here, and here. You can see the lighter squares where the objects stood."

"He's stolen them!" charged Granny, pointing her cane toward Mr. Boggs and nearly losing her balance in her distress at finding everything so forlorn. She needed the cane more for walking than she did for pointing.

"Maybe he has," Honey, who helped steady her, was heard to whisper.

"They're stored away," Mr. Boggs defended himself, "to keep them safe. It was the master's order."

"Can you tell us what used to be here, Mrs. Joerg?" asked Peter.

"Certainly I can," she assured him. "I remember exactly the way it was when this fellow first started to work here. Everything was in order then, but what a place it is now! Not a painting on the wall and not a rug on the floor! All the cubbyholes empty of statues, and even the weapons gone from the walls!"

"What weapons?" asked Judy.

"A shield with the Dent coat of arms hung about here." Again she pointed with her cane. "There were crossed spears above the mirror that hung on this wall, and I remember a battle axe, a sword, and another shield."

"Didn't you say something before about velvets and tapestries, and a suit of armor?"

Granny nodded.

"It stood in the corner just as you go upstairs. A fine suit of armor it was, too, with a tall plumed helmet and gauntlets of gold—"

"Our man from Mars!" Honey exclaimed in a whisper that drew more hushed exclamations from Lois and Lorraine. Granny, apparently, did not hear them. She glanced into the desolate ballroom where, she said, the Dent girls used to have gay parties, and quickly drew back.

The dining hall was equally barren. Not a table or a chair remained. The great oak sideboard stood bare and empty. Granny commented sadly on the missing glassware and china.

"Nothing is left! Nothing!" she lamented as she was helped up the winding stairway toward the master's quarters, as Mr. Boggs called the rooms in the tower. "John must be dead. Oh, that I should live to see the castle robbed and me helpless!"

"Helpless!" Peter chuckled. "I only wish there were more people as helpful. Now, Mr. Boggs, that armor Mrs. Joerg mentioned. You wouldn't have it in your room, would you?"

"It's stored away," the man began.

But Granny interrupted furiously.

"Stored away, is it? Where, then? Where is everything stored? What kind of lies are you telling us, Hiram Boggs?"

"It's the truth," he returned without a change of expression. "I follow the master's orders."

"But if a man is ill, how can he give proper orders?" asked Emil Joerg.

A smile crossed the caretaker's face as he replied,

"His mind is perfectly clear even though he's eighty-four."

"That's young!" snapped Granny. She waited a moment to catch her breath, as they had now reached the top of the winding stone stairway. Mr. Boggs was ahead.

"Here it is, sir," he said to Peter, stopping before a closed door on which was tacked a large printed sign:

PLEASE DO NOT DISTURB

"You see," he continued, "he must be sleeping."

"For keeps, maybe," Emil Joerg muttered.

"How can he hang out the sign if he's a helpless cripple?" asked Judy.

"At his request," the caretaker explained carefully, "I placed it there."

"At my request," snapped Peter, "you're taking it down. Is the door locked?"

"Always—"

"Where's the key?"

"He has it. He can reach the door from his bed—"

"Hold on there!" Peter stopped him. "You have a key to this room and I want you to tell me where it is."

"In my room," the man admitted unwillingly. "Here, right next to the master's."

He indicated a room which Peter quickly entered. It did not take Mr. Boggs long to find the key.

Meantime Granny was growing hysterical. Banging on the oak panel of the locked door, she cried, "John! John! Let us in! Can you hear me, John? It's Hilma Joerg who used to take care of you when you were a baby. John!"

She was sobbing brokenly with her head against the door panel when Peter and the caretaker returned with the key. Then her sobs stopped suddenly. She listened for a tense few moments and then, turning to Hiram Boggs, said flatly, "He's dead. You've killed him!"

"Just a moment," Peter warned, stepping between them as the old lady raised her cane to strike the caretaker. "We have the key. Open the door, please, Judy, but don't be surprised at what you find. The man may be dead."

"Not him," Boggs said, forgetting his careful English. "He's a sound sleeper, though. I have strict orders not to disturb him when he's sleeping."

"Right now," Granny said dryly, "you're taking orders from Uncle Sam, and don't you forget it."

"She's right, Boggs. Don't make a move," Peter ordered.

Judy's hand was trembling as she inserted the large brass key in the lock. It made a groaning sound as she turned it and swung open the door. Mr. Boggs was smiling.

"There you see, sir, sleeping—"

He broke off suddenly. The room was fully, even elaborately furnished. But the huge old canopied bed was empty. So was the chair beside it. A meal on the bedside table was only half eaten. A cup of coffee poured from the little silver pot that stood on the tray had been allowed to grow cold. A shimmering glass of red gelatine had remained untouched. The tray looked as if it had been hastily pushed aside when something unexpected happened. But what? Judy couldn't guess. She only knew that John Dent simply wasn't there.

"He's gone!" Granny wailed, staring at the empty bed. "Poor John is gone and you've kept it from me, Hiram Boggs. How long has he been dead?"

The caretaker seemed no less surprised than Granny to find the bed empty. He opened his mouth to say something, but no words came. Finally he managed to stammer, "He's t-tricked me! He's gone all right, but he's not dead!"

"Where is he then?" Granny demanded. "If he was up and able to be about, he'd be fixing for the party he promised me, but what place is this for a party? And who wants a party with the twins gone and, like as not, dead too! Only Emil is left to me, and him likely not for long. There is a curse on me—that I must live to see all my loved ones die!"

Nobody could stop Granny's sobbing, although Judy tried to tell her that the caretaker had made up the story to frighten her.

"Oh, dear Lord," she moaned, "let me die, too!"

At that, poor Granny went all to pieces. Honey saw what was happening and cried out in sudden alarm.

"Oh, Judy! Quick! She's going to faint!"

CHAPTER XIX

"If This Is a Dungeon"

IT WAS true. Granny had reached the end of her resources. If Judy had not been standing beside her she might have fallen, with what tragic results it was easy to imagine. Her amazing energy was at a low ebb now.

"Granny!" cried Emil, bending over her after he had helped place her flat on the canopied bed.

Granny was pitifully thin and light. Her pulse was beating with a faint flutter that might stop at any moment. A silent prayer was in Judy's heart as she went into action, doing what her father would have done if he had been there.

"We'll need water," she said.

Fortunately, a big white pitcher of water stood on a near-by washstand. Lorraine brought towels and dipped them in the water. Honey even found smelling salts on the dresser. With everybody working over her, Granny slowly began to regain consciousness.

The cool water, the loosened clothing, and a breeze from the narrow window Emil had flung open were taking effect. First a moan and then a fluttering eyelid told Judy they had won the battle. Emil, big man that he was, burst into tears.

"Don't scare us like this again, Granny!" he sobbed. "You know how we need you."

Granny's head turned a little.

"It's all over for me," she sighed. "Only take care of yourself, Emil."

"I'll take care of you, Granny." His big hand closed over her wrinkled one. "I need you more than ever with my kids gone. You can't leave me in all this trouble."

Granny moaned again.

"You've got a good wife—"

"A heartbroken wife," Emil interrupted. "I told her to stay close to the house and keep calling. Maybe the kids will come back by themselves."

"Back from where?" Granny was growing excited again. "They were here at the castle. I know it!"

"It's a lie!" interrupted Hiram Boggs, but got no further. Peter silenced him.

All this time Granny's eyes had been closed. Now they snapped open. When she saw where she was she made a feeble attempt to sit up, but was eased gently back on the pillow.

"The dungeon!" she moaned. "John could tell you—"

"We'll find him," Emil assured her. "If he could climb out of bed and leave his food half eaten he must be playing tricks on somebody."

"Don't blame him too quickly," warned Peter.

Judy noticed how close he had been keeping to the caretaker's side. Evidently Peter suspected Mr. Boggs knew who the real culprit was if he could only get the truth from him. Had John Dent tricked him or was it the other way around?

"The dungeon!" Granny repeated feebly.

Peter came closer.

"Go on, Mrs. Joerg."

"I know there is one," she said, "but they closed it off years ago. Used to be a station of the underground railroad."

"But that was in Civil War times!" exclaimed Lois. "You can't remember that far back, can you, Mrs. Joerg?"

This brought a new light to her eyes.

"Course I can remember. I was a little girl living here in the castle. The Dents were good to me and took me in after my father died. What fun Debby and I used to have pretending we were princesses! That was before John was born. If I could see him once more . . ."

Her voice drifted off into dreams of the past.

"You will," Peter promised. "We'll find him and the twins, too. I imagine they're together, wherever they are."

"Of course," agreed Judy. "They must be together. They said they were going to find their uncle John and they probably did. Now it's up to us to find them."

"Then go! Don't mind me," begged Granny. "I'm no good any more. A hundred years is too long—"

"You haven't reached a hundred yet, but we mean to see that you do, don't we, girls?"

"We certainly do," cried Lois and Lorraine.

"I'm used to taking care of my grandparents," Honey began, "but if I stay here I can't help Judy and Peter search the castle—"

"We'll stay," Lois offered. "I'm not sure we want to help search, anyway. We'll be together here and if Mrs. Joerg needs anything we know what to do. Don't we, Lorraine?" Lois asked.

"Is is safe?" Judy whispered to Peter.

"Nothing's safe," he replied grimly, "but we can't leave her alone. See this rope? It must be a bell cord. Pull it, Lois, if you need us."

"Does it work?" Judy asked.

Peter tried it and a great clanging sound echoed throughout the gloomy old castle.

"It works all right," he said, and rang it again.

"Why, that was what we heard!" exclaimed Judy. "Remember that crash at the end of the violin playing? Someone must have been here around noon when we heard it. Maybe we can find the violin, too."

"Was someone here?" Peter asked the caretaker.

"It must have been the master," he replied, a little sullenly, Judy thought, "ringing for his dinner. When I got back I brought it up to him. There it is still on the tray. I'll save his dessert for him. He didn't finish—"

"I'll take that," Peter interrupted.

The dessert glass of red gelatine looked innocent enough to Judy, but something must have made Peter suspicious of it. As he started to take it, Mr. Boggs deliberately tipped the tray and sent it flying.

"Oh," cried Honey in swift pain as a sliver of glass hit her ankle. It stung for only a minute. The other girls were already gathering up the pieces. Judy managed to save most of the gelatine, scooping it up in an empty tobacco tin she discovered under the bed.

Peter stared hard at the caretaker. "You expected John Dent to eat this gelatine and then have a nice long sleep, didn't you, Boggs?" he said. "Somebody gave you the sleeping medicine you couldn't get from Dr. Bolton."

Mr. Boggs deliberately tipped the tray

"It was to quiet his nerves," the caretaker insisted. "He was always complaining of the pain in his leg. I thought he couldn't use it, but I was mistaken. It won't take him far, though. He must be somewhere near the castle."

"Wearing armor?" Judy whispered to Peter. "Do you think that's his secret?"

"More likely Boggs was wearing it, but it's a thought," Peter whispered back. "Where are the furnishings from the entrance hall?" he asked in a louder voice. "Didn't you say you'd stored them somewhere, Mr. Boggs?"

"I did." His reply was as quick as it was unexpected. "I stored them in the dungeon."

Judy and Peter looked at each other in dismay. This dashed their hopes of finding the children there.

"We'll have a look," Peter said finally. Attempting a lightheartedness he did not feel, he turned to his sister and said, "If Judy and I don't come right back, just look for us in the dungeon."

"Are you serious?" Honey asked. "I won't look for you in the dungeon. I'll be there with you."

"What's this about the dungeon?" asked Emil Joerg. "Have you found out where it is?"

"No," Peter said, "but I intend to. Want to come?"

"Sure do," the twins' father replied.

"We'll search this room while you're exploring the rest of the castle," Lois offered. "Granny's asleep, bless her heart! But we won't leave her."

"Good!" approved Judy. "Don't be surprised at what you find, though. I peeked under the bed when we were picking up that glass, and there are a lot of things under there."

"No bodies, I hope?"

"Oh, Lois! How can you?" cried Lorraine. "There really might be."

"Not a chance," Peter said, "but you might find a violin."

"I'll look for it," Lois promised.

Judy turned to Lorraine.

"What about you? Are you still afraid?"

"Scared to death," she admitted, "but that's what I expect when I go anywhere with you. Arthur warned me over the telephone. He said he'd come for us in his car if we weren't home by ten."

Peter consulted his watch.

"It's nearly that now."

"Arthur doesn't approve of escapades like this. He isn't like your brother," Lois added.

"Don't I know it!" exclaimed Judy. "He isn't like Peter, either. Well, let's start on our tour of the castle. Mr. Boggs has promised to lead us to the dungeon and I'm afraid he means it. 'Bye, you brave little Florence Nightingales!"

Lois giggled.

"You've got it wrong, Judy. Mr. Boggs is carrying the lamp."

It was really a lantern which he held aloft as the searching party descended the circular stone stairway leading down from the tower. They passed through the entrance hall, the dining hall, and from there to a narrow passageway that seemed to be built between the double walls of the castle. Stonework rose high on either side. The sky, now dotted with stars and bright with moonlight, was the ceiling. Judy looked up at it and felt better. The stars were always the same. This thought comforted her.

"Look up there," she said. "Honey, don't you love it?"

"Yes," sighed Honey. "I wish Horace—"

"Watch it!" Peter interrupted. "There's a loose stone there somewhere. You girls hadn't better indulge in any more star-gazing. Just watch your feet and hurry along as fast as you can!"

The warning came too late. Judy would have hurried, but she had already tripped on one of the stones. As she bent to try to move it back in place she found herself gazing into a deep black hole.

"Peter!" she called. "Honey! Come here! If this is a dungeon . . ."

CHAPTER XX

Trapped!

"What is it?" cried Honey, hurrying to Judy's side. "Have you really found the dungeon? I thought this was it. I thought—"

"Think again, Honey!" Judy interrupted. "That lovely long passageway with the stars for a ceiling couldn't be called a dungeon. It's this! It must be. Have you got the flashlight? There! Can you see what I see?"

"A ladder!" Honey exclaimed as the light played around on the rungs and showed her what it was. "Oh dear! It looks as if it went down forever. What do you suppose is at the bottom?"

Judy shivered.

"I don't know, but I suppose we'll have to find out."

She herself was none too eager to descend into the black hole she had discovered. There was something terrifying about it. She thought of John Dent and then remembered that he had been very much alive when he rang for his midday dinner. Why had he left it in such a hurry? Did Hiram Boggs really believe he was a cripple? Had the twins found him and, if so, where were they now? Surely, Judy told herself, this was her opportunity to explore whatever secrets the castle held.

"Where's Peter?" she asked, a new doubt assailing her. "I called both of you, but he didn't come back."

"He couldn't. He went on ahead without us. He had to," Honey explained. "Mr. Boggs was almost running. He may be trying to escape."

"I don't think he will. Peter will see that he doesn't get away. He suspects the gelatine and I think there's even more that he hasn't told me. I know I've figured out a few things I haven't told him."

"For instance?"

"It's about the purchase money. It isn't quite sorted out in my mind I wanted Peter's help on it. We promised each other we wouldn't get separated."

"It can't be helped, I'm afraid. We are separated already, Judy. You and I are here," Honey pointed out. "Lois and Lorraine are upstairs with Granny. Peter and Emil Joerg are somewhere farther down this long passageway following Boggs to wherever he's taking them. If it's to the dungeon, I don't know what this is. Some day he will find out, as I did, that lies never get anyone out of trouble—only deeper into it."

"If anyone gets deeper into trouble it will be us," Judy said ruefully. "I mean if we descend into this pit without letting Peter know where we are."

"That's right," Honey agreed apprehensively. "We may run into almost anything."

"You mean our man from Mars? I wouldn't be afraid of him," declared Judy. "We know now that it was only someone dressed up in a suit of armor."

"Yes, but who was it?"

"If it was Mr. Boggs, he isn't dressed up in it any more. As for John Dent, I wouldn't object to finding him, would you?"

"It might be a gruesome find."

"Oh, Honey!" Judy said impatiently. "You always imagine the worst. If we find anything it will probably be all that stuff Mr. Boggs said he stored in the dungeon, the suit of armor and everything."

This won Honey over.

"All right, let's look," she said. "But I still think it's dangerous. Even if we could put the stone back in place we might trap ourselves where no one could find us. And if we leave the hole open someone may fall into it. I know," Honey exclaimed, the artist in her coming to their aid. "We'll post a danger sign. I'll letter it. Luckily, I have a Wolf pencil I brought from the studio. But what'll we use for paper?"

"I saw an old cardboard carton back there. I'll get it," Judy offered.

In a very few minutes Honey had the sign all lettered. Judy gazed at it in amusement. It said:

DANGER! GIRLS AT WORK

and below, in smaller letters, Honey wrote, *We are exploring the dungeon.*

She signed her name below that.

"And now," she announced, "as soon as you've signed your name, Judy, I'm ready to descend with you into the depths of the earth. I hope this ladder's strong!"

"I'll go down first with the flashlight while you pull the box in place over the hole," Judy said.

This done, the danger of the adventure was forgotten in the fun of climbing down, down, down!

"It goes to China," complained Honey. "I hope the Chinese are friendly."

"Me, too," giggled Judy. "I think we're nearly to the bottom. I hope I don't drop the flashlight. We're going to need it down here."

"I see the floor now. It's just dirt like any hole," Honey said in disappointment.

Judy laughed.

"What did you expect? Marble?"

Honey did not answer. She was concentrating all her attention on the path of the flashlight which danced weirdly this way and that through the inky blackness.

The dungeon appeared to be one large room walled in on all sides with stone. It had been used as a store-house for all sorts of things which the girls now in-spected. Judy, handing the flashlight to Honey, threw open the lid of an old trunk to find it filled with silks and velvets of another era.

"These can't be the draperies from the windows. Why, they're dresses!" She held one up. "Imagine anyone wearing this! Wouldn't you just die in all this heavy velvet and a lace yoke up to your ears? Let's take off our coats and try some on."

"I think I need my coat," Honey said with a shiver. "It's cold down here. It was chilly up there, but this is worse. Don't you suppose there's any way to let in a little light?"

"It's night. Remember?"

"People must be getting worried at home. Grandma and Grandpa think I've just gone for a ride, but Horace—"

"He should be worried," declared Judy. "He got us into this. Look, Honey! Here's another quaint old dress. Who do you suppose used to wear these things?"

"Who do you suppose used to wear these things?"

"Maybe the Dent girls."

"Or Granny. Just think!" Judy exclaimed. "This was used as a station of the underground railway in Civil War times, and she remembers as far back as that! How wonderful!"

"And how sad," Honey added, "if the birthday most people never live to see has to be spoiled by—by tragedy."

"I don't believe it will be," Judy replied. "If the twins found their uncle and helped him escape from the castle, it was no tragedy. I'm convinced Hiram Boggs had him imprisoned in his room and the twins let him out. You can see just how it happened. He was playing his violin when we arrived at the castle this morning. That crash we heard at the end was when he rang for his dinner."

"But Mr. Boggs was away then," Honey objected. "He was visiting your father and trying to get him to prescribe sleeping medicine. You told me."

"You're right," agreed Judy. "I guess I'm getting too tired to think straight. He couldn't have heard him ring. He didn't bring his dinner until after he returned, and by then the twins had found him and helped him escape—"

"No," laughed Honey. "He was eating his dinner when whatever it was happened."

"Then that theory's no good," Judy admitted. "Maybe they found him while he was eating."

"Or maybe Mr. Boggs found them!"

"Oh, Honey! I'm afraid he did. That's what I've been afraid of all along," confessed Judy. "The twins found something he wanted behind that stone in the wall. Maybe it was the purchase money—the purchase money," Judy repeated in a whisper. It was such an important theory that she felt she had to whisper. "I meant to tell Peter," she added. "That gold piece he has in his pocket may be part of it. You see, it could have been hidden behind that stone with the wooden panel in back of it. Flash your light this way, Honey! There! That proves at least one of my theories was right. What do you see?"

"A door!" Honey exclaimed. "Oh, Judy! There's another way out of here. We don't have to climb up that long ladder. We can just open the door."

"It may not be that simple," Judy said. "I suspect that door has been closed for a long, long time. Perhaps ever since the Civil War. It may be hard to open."

Honey tried, and found it impossible.

"It's no use, Honey. The door is locked. Even if we could open it," Judy continued, "if it leads where I think it does, it's walled up on the other side. There's just one loose stone in the wall. It must have been the panel of this door that we saw behind it."

"Then no one could open it?"

"Peter and I couldn't today." Another thought

came to Judy and she added, "But a lot may have happened since then. If this is the way our man from Mars went through the wall—"

"Do you think it could be?" Honey interrupted hopefully.

"I don't know what to think," replied Judy, "but it is the only theory that makes sense. If it's true, we may find his armor stored here."

"We'll have plenty of time to look for it," Honey said, and Judy realized that her voice sounded strange. "Judy, somebody's taken away the ladder while we were looking at the dress-up clothes!"

CHAPTER XXI

The Armored Knight

AT FIRST Judy thought Honey must be joking. Was the ladder really gone? Were they buried deep under the castle in this terrible place? Then Honey beamed the flashlight on the spot where the ladder should have been, and she knew for a certainty that it was true. Honey had a queer, dazed look on her face.

"How could they have done it?" she asked at last. "Wouldn't we have heard them?"

"Apparently we didn't. We were laughing and fooling around. Whoever pulled up the ladder managed to do it very quietly. But why didn't Peter stop him?" asked Judy.

"You think Mr. Boggs did it, don't you?" Honey questioned weakly.

"Who else? He must have tricked Peter. Maybe he did get away."

"I don't think so. Listen, Judy! Was that a shot?"

Judy's face went white. The two girls clung to each other for a moment. Then Judy said, "I'm afraid it was. Maybe the police have come. They'll find us. They'll *have* to. There really isn't anything for us to do until they come."

"We could search the place," Honey ventured.

"All right," Judy agreed without too much enthusiasm. "We'll begin systematically and work our way around. With you to hold the flashlight and me to search, we ought to turn up something."

Honey sent a flash of light along the back wall. Curiously, the walls had been left free of objects, although the rest of the cavern was strewn with all sorts of things. Then Judy realized it was because the walls were made of stone. What had been thrown into the dungeon had, in most cases, gone in the center. A dark object loomed up.

"What is it?" gasped Honey.

"Not our man from Mars. Only a hatrack. There's a marble-topped dresser beyond it. Someone has made a pretty thorough search for something," observed Judy. "All the drawers are pulled open and the stuff is half out of them. Eeek!"

This exclamation came when Judy withdrew an old feather boa that wriggled and writhed like a snake. It seemed to be yards long.

"Don't try it on," Honey warned her. "It may have moths in it."

"Not a chance," Judy said. "The place reeks with moth balls. We could play marbles with them to pass the time."

"I thought time disintegrated them."

"The moth balls? It does. I haven't found them yet, but I can tell by the smell that fresh ones have been put down here just recently. Those crates along the wall are reeking with them. I suppose they're filled with old clothes, too."

"I suppose so," agreed Honey. "We'd need a hammer to open them."

"If we had a hammer," Judy said, "I wouldn't use it to open crates. I'd hammer my way out of here. You don't see any tools of any kind, do you?"

"Not yet. I don't see any of those things Mr. Boggs said he put in storage, either," Honey remarked as they searched among more relics. "Everything here is old and cobwebby."

Judy shivered. "I hope spiders don't come with the cobwebs. We may have to spend the night here."

"There's a bed."

Honey's light played on an old coiled bedspring that stood against the last wall. They had made a complete circle of the room, and still no one had come to release them. The air in the dungeon was becoming oppressive. There were no windows and only the one unyielding door.

"We could scream for help. Do you think it would do any good?" asked Honey.

"I don't know," replied Judy, "but let's try it, anyway. Together, now! Hel-lp! Hel-lp!"

Up and up went the scream, bouncing back at them with a fearful echo. Nothing they had experienced was quite as terrifying as this, for here in the dungeon the echo was all around them, not only from the four walls but from above as well.

"Let's not try that again," Judy exclaimed when the echoes had subsided.

Honey was shivering. "What will we do?"

"We might pull that bed down and get a little rest," replied Judy. "We could cover it with some of the old-time dresses and it would be quite comfy. I'm beginning to ache all over."

"Maybe you've caught Horace's virus."

"No, I'm just tired," Judy sighed. "I know the feeling. I never thought when Peter and I set out for the castle this morning that I'd be spending the night in a dungeon with you, Honey. I hope you'll forgive me."

"Silly!" Honey laughed affectionately. "It's not your fault."

Judy's answer was a yawn. Her eyes were suddenly heavy with weariness. It did not occur to her that it might be caused by lack of air until Honey leaned against her.

"Does your head ache?" she asked. "Mine is splitting. When are we going to get out of this awful place? It must be nearly midnight. Are you wearing your watch?"

"My what?"

"Your watch. Judy!" exclaimed Honey in sudden panic. "You frighten me when you shut your eyes like that. Wake up and tell me what time it is."

The flashlight in her eyes roused Judy from the drowsiness that had all but overcome her. She looked at her wrist watch and exclaimed, "It's past midnight. What a shame! Tomorrow is Granny's birthday."

"I'm going to be too tired to go to her party if she has one. Can't we pull down the bed, Judy? We're both going to sleep standing up."

"What we need is air, not a place to sleep," declared Judy. "If we pulled down the bed in this stuffy hole we might go to sleep and not wake up. I mean it, Honey! We'll have to find some way out of here and what way is there except that door?"

"You said it was all walled up on the other side."

"I know," Judy agreed, "but there was one loose stone. It would let in a little air if we pushed it out. We'll have to get the door down first. If we could find a knife or a screwdriver, I believe I could take it off its hinges."

"Could you do it with shears? There's a great big pair of shears in the top drawer of that dresser," Honey remembered.

They found them quickly.

"Just the thing!" Judy exclaimed. "Let me have a little more light on the door. And start calling for help again. It'll keep you awake."

Honey obeyed, though her voice sounded drowsy. A moment later she dropped the flashlight. It rolled, making weird circles of light dance for a moment like demons. Then it blinked and went out.

"I couldn't help it," moaned Honey.

"I know," Judy soothed her, trying not to show the panic she felt. "A little air is coming in through the crack in the door. Breathe deep, Honey! There's a little light coming in, too. I didn't notice it before with the flashlight on. Where do you suppose it's coming from?"

"The moon," Honey murmured.

Fantastic as it sounded, Judy soon discovered that it was true. There wasn't a glimmer of light at the sides of the door, but at the bottom where the crack was wider there was a definite glow that proved but one thing.

"It isn't walled in on the other side any more! It can't be!" exclaimed Judy. "Listen! What's that?"

The sound proved to be the turning of a key in the lock. Judy dropped the scissors. They were no longer needed. She shook Honey, bringing her back to full consciousness. Slowly the door opened, letting in a shaft of moonlight. Outside, everything looked strange, somehow, as though they had been transported to another planet. Both girls made a dash through the doorway. Then a queer sound, as of someone laughing, made Judy turn her head.

"The man from Mars!" she gasped. "*He* opened the door."

The alarming figure before her stood perfectly still while her incredulous gaze swept from his plumed helmet to the spurs on his plated boots. His entire suit was made of metal plates resembling scales and jointed like a lobster's tail. She jumped back, uttering a sharp cry as the mailed arms reached toward her with mechanical precision.

"Who—are—you?" she managed to gasp.

"Run, Judy run!" Honey was screaming hysterically.

At that very moment, another sound came, this time behind them.

"Judy! Honey!" a voice called from the depths of the dungeon.

"It's Peter! He's let down the ladder and come for us at last!" exclaimed Judy.

"We're being rescued from all sides. I don't know which way to turn," Honey declared, and began to laugh helplessly.

There was no doubt in Judy's mind. She rushed

toward Peter. Murmuring something meant for his ears alone, she let him hold her so tightly she could not have turned back even if she had wanted to.

Lights were flashing now, penetrating the darkest corners. Behind Peter were several men, one of them a state trooper and another Peter's superior, David Trent. They were talking in excited tones about having discovered the hideout. Whose hideout, Judy and Honey wondered. In their eagerness to tell their own adventures they managed to make everything still more confusing. Suddenly Honey, who had followed Judy back into the dungeon, exclaimed:

"Where is he? Oh, Judy! He's gone! And we didn't find out a thing about him!"

CHAPTER XXII

The Greatest Gift

"Who's gone?" asked Peter as he walked out into the moonlight with Judy on one arm and Honey on the other. Judy saw the pile of stones someone had removed, and realized that this was the same path they had followed to the blank wall.

"Our knight in shining armor. He frightened me half to death," Judy admitted, "and then you came and it didn't matter—"

"Dearest," Peter whispered, brushing her hair with his lips.

"Don't you care?" asked Judy, looking up at him in surprise. "If it was John Dent who opened the door, maybe he knows where the twins are."

"Maybe," Peter said, "but I doubt it. Their mother knows where they are, though, and so does their father. They're right where we all ought to be. Sound asleep in their beds."

"You're joking!" Honey charged.

But Judy saw that Peter was serious. One excited question followed another.

"Where were they? How did they get home? Tell us about it!" both girls demanded.

To most of their questions, Peter answered, "We'll know more about it in the morning."

"But it's morning now," Judy protested, "and to-morrow is Granny's birthday—"

"Which makes it all the more important for you girls to get a little sleep so you can help with plans for her party," Peter interrupted.

"Will it be in the castle?" asked Honey.

"We don't know," Peter replied. "There's a lot we don't know. We haven't found John Dent yet. The police arrived a few minutes after you girls disappeared, to say the twins had come home by themselves, but we don't know where they had been. They were too tired to talk. The policeman I spoke to said they told him nothing but fairy tales."

"I'd like to hear them," declared Judy.

"You shall in the morning."

"What about Granny? Does she know?"

"Yes, we woke her up to tell her. Your father came

and gave her something for her heart, but she said he'd given her all the heart medicine she needed when he told her that the twins were safe."

"I see what she meant. Does Dad know we've been rescued from the dungeon? Did Horace come, too? There's plenty of news for him if he's well enough—"

"Yes to everything," Peter replied before Judy had finished asking the questions. "Horace brought Blackberry. Actually," Peter continued in the quiet voice he always used when he had something important to say, "it was Blackberry who found you. We saw him sniffing around that loose stone before we lifted it up. The ladder wasn't beside it. Boggs had some idea of using it to escape over the castle wall. Funny, neither of you has asked me about him."

"We were afraid to," confessed Judy. "We heard that shot."

"Yes, he tried to get away. That's why I didn't come back for you girls when you first called. He turned a corner and ducked into a niche in the wall and I ran right past him. It must have been then that he came back and pulled up the ladder."

"He must have disposed of the sign I lettered, too," Honey put in. "We thought someone might fall into the dungeon if we didn't post a warning."

"We found the sign thrown in a corner. We knew Boggs must have removed it. He even put the stone back in place. It's a good thing the police came when they did," declared Peter. "They'll get the truth out of him before daylight."

Judy doubted it, but she didn't say so. Suddenly she remembered Lois and Lorraine and asked about them.

"Arthur came for them," Peter told her.

"My goodness!" Honey exclaimed. "Did everybody come? I didn't realize we were in the dungeon that long."

"You were there all of two hours, and what an anxious time it was for all of us!"

"Two wasted hours," Judy lamented. "We didn't find a thing."

It was daylight before Judy discovered the importance of what she had found. By then the crates stored along the walls of the dungeon had been opened and definitely identified as the shipment of woolens hijacked along the turnpike the week before. Peter told Judy all about it while Mrs. Bolton bustled around fixing them a very special breakfast.

"To make up for the dinner you missed," she declared.

Judy had fallen asleep in the car on the way back from the castle and hadn't had a thing to eat since she and Honey were rescued from the dungeon. Peter had slept a little, too, but Horace had stayed up ever since he got back home. He came in, heavy-eyed, while Judy and Peter were still at breakfast.

"It isn't the virus, it's the Sand Man that's got me

now," he said as he sank into a chair and tossed the first edition of the *Farringdon Daily Herald* on the table. The headlines ran:

MASTER OF CASTLE MISSING

and went on to tell a fabulous story of how the mysterious recluse had been alternately terrorized and cared for by the criminal Hiram Boggs until he became suspicious of the man's intentions and hid in a suit of armor to watch him.

There was also a news item about Granny. As Judy read it she grew more and more puzzled.

"It's exciting," she agreed, "and mysterious. But haven't you taken a big chance making wild guesses about John Dent and reporting things before they happen?"

"What things?" Horace asked innocently.

"Granny's party," replied Judy. "You say a hundred guests will gather in the castle to celebrate the one hundredth birthday of Lars Olsen's daughter, Hilma Joerg. The picture's nice. You've reported accurately from the notes I took. But where will you get a hundred people, and how do you know John Dent will allow them to gather at the castle, and what sort of a place is it for a party, anyway, with all the furnishings gone?"

"They aren't," Horace replied, answering Judy's last question first. "Mother found them."

Mrs. Bolton smiled. "Yes, Judy girl, for once, your mother has helped you solve one of your mysteries. You see, I knew the woman who was going to be Mrs. Boggs."

"Mrs. Boggs!" Judy exclaimed. "I didn't know there was one."

"There wasn't—quite. They were going to be married, but she broke their engagement because of his violent temper. She was the one who told me what little I knew about him. You see, until they broke up and she moved away, he kept showering her with presents for the home he had bought. It is one of those old houses downtown. The castle furnishings must have looked well in it. She knew nothing about their having been stolen," Judy's mother went on. "Mr. Boggs made up some story about an uncle who was supposed to have died and left him the things. When the police went to the house last night, they found it all."

"Mother, that's wonderful!" Judy exclaimed. "Well, Hiram Boggs probably is making up some fast stories to tell the police right now."

Horace grinned. So did Peter.

"No," Peter said. "Boggs is telling the truth. He saw us plant the parrot's cage, but he didn't know what it was. Mr. Trent borrowed it at my suggestion and hid it down at headquarters. Boggs thinks it's a clever new invention, some sort of lie detector—"

Judy nearly choked on her coffee.

"A lie detector!" she exclaimed. "Oh, Peter, how funny! Did he really tell you the truth?"

"I think he did. He admits that his main purpose in taking the job of caretaker at the castle was to search for the missing purchase money. He is convinced that John Dent has it hidden somewhere. For nearly two years now, Boggs has been giving John Dent sleeping medicine in his food so that the search could safely be carried on. Recently, though, John Dent must have become suspicious, and so he began to play a few tricks of his own on the caretaker. Boggs told us he has heard violin music from time to time but never saw anyone playing. And he's convinced that the castle is haunted by a ghost in armor—so you see, it couldn't have been Boggs whom you saw last night."

"Goodness!" Judy exclaimed. "Then Mr. Boggs really believed the stories he was spreading about the castle being haunted."

Peter nodded. "Yes. Actually," he went on, "I think Boggs is a bit crazy. Hijacking that truckload of woolens was a stupid thing to do. He didn't know how to dispose of the loot when he got it, so he stowed it down in the dungeon. And stripping the castle of all its furnishings—he might have known the stuff would all be located sooner or later, and traced to him. The prize boner of all, though, was when he captured the twins and shut them up in the dungeon. Evidently he was becoming desperate because he couldn't locate the money. Anyway, he had some idea of holding them for ransom and forcing John Dent to turn over the purchase money to him in order to get the twins back."

"Just how did the twins escape?" Judy demanded.

"They told us they were rescued by a knight in armor who came through the door in the wall," Peter said.

"Whoever the knight is, he's friendly," Judy observed. "He helped us escape, too."

"Perhaps that was a different knight," said Horace.

"You mean there are two of them? I give up," declared Judy. "Maybe it *was* an invasion from Mars, and the Martians aren't as warlike as people suppose. I wonder what the twins will say about it. When do we meet them?"

"Whenever you say—"

"It can't be too soon to suit me," declared Judy, finishing her breakfast in a hurry and grabbing her leopard coat. "It's a little warm for a fur coat today," she explained, "but the twins will know me in it."

An hour later, she and Peter were meeting the children at the castle gate. Their mother was with them.

"They can't wait to see Granny," young Mrs. Joerg

explained, smiling. "She spent the night at the castle."

"We know," Peter told her. "We spent most of it there ourselves." Quickly he reported what they had discovered so far, telling her how Judy's mother had helped locate the missing furniture. "Mrs. Bolton will be here later to help. There'll be a lot to do," he added. "The moving men will put the heavy stuff back in place, but you ladies will want to arrange the draperies and get ready for the party."

At the word *party* the twins' eyes grew round. They began hopping up and down, chanting, "There's going to be a party! For Granny, for Granny!"

"Indeed there is," their mother agreed. "I didn't know how we'd manage it, but with you people to help—"

"We'll help too!" the twins interrupted. "Uncle John said it was all right. He told us not to worry about him. He said he'd be here to help celebrate."

"He did say that? When?" asked Peter. "When did you see him?"

"After we saw you under the tree," the boy replied. "The branch we were on broke, and Erna and I fell out of the tree."

"But we weren't hurted," Erna put in proudly.

"No, we weren't," Emil continued. "We went up the path to where the letters are on the wall, and we saw an arrow pointing to one of the stones—"

"And we dug around the stone until we got it out," Erna took up the story, "and behind it—"

"Let me tell it," Emil interrupted. "We found a big box full of gold and money. Granny needs money, so we thought we'd wrap it up and give it to her for a present."

"But the box was too heavy for us to carry," Erna said, "so we hid it in the bushes. And then we went back and climbed the tree and got over the wall and went into the castle."

"Erna didn't want to," the boy explained. "She was afraid Mr. Boggs would catch us, because we knew he was back. We saw his car. But I made her, and we went upstairs—"

"And Emil opened a door," the little girl took it up excitedly, "and who do you think we found! Uncle John!"

"That's right," Emil said. "He was sitting up in bed, eating his dinner. We told him about Granny's birthday, and the present we had for her, and he said we should go right ahead and plan the party, and he would, too. But when we looked for the present this morning," the boy finished mournfully, "we couldn't find it any more."

"It's losted," Erna chimed in, "and now we can't give Granny anything."

Judy and Peter looked at each other.

"You saved my coat from Mr. Boggs," she said

slowly, "but he may not have come off empty-handed after all."

Peter turned to the children. "You say you told your uncle John about the present," he said. "Did you tell him where you had left it?"

"Yes," said the boy. "And he promised he would keep it a secret. That was just before old man Boggs came in and caught us."

"He was awful mean," the little girl told them, her eyes round at the memory. "He told Uncle John he was going to take us away and Uncle John would never see us again if he didn't give up the purchase money."

"We knew he meant our present for Granny," Emil explained, "so we were glad Uncle John had promised he wouldn't tell anybody about it."

"What happened then?" Peter prompted the children quietly.

"Old man Boggs took us way downstairs to a hole with a ladder in it," the boy said, "and made us go down the ladder into a dungeon!"

"O-o-oh, we were scared!" little Erna squealed. "We yelled for help all afternoon, but nobody heard us——"

"And then the knight in armor came through the door in the wall and let us out," Emil went on, "and outside, it was night, so we ran home as fast as we could."

"We were so glad to get home," the little girl said, and added sadly, "If only we could have brought Granny's present with us."

Judy hugged them both impulsively.

"We may find it, but even if we don't," she told them in a whisper that made it sound like an important secret, "you're giving her yourselves alive and well. Whatever else you give her, she'll like that best of all."

CHAPTER XXIII

One Hundred Candles

It took the twins a moment to figure out what Judy meant. Then Emil said, "Granny's alive still and she's a hundred—almost. And we're alive."

Erna, too, seemed deeply impressed by the wonder of being alive. She was quiet for all of a minute.

"The police wouldn't believe us when we told them, but there is a knight at the castle," declared Emil. "A real knight just like in story books."

"Don't you think the knight might have been your uncle John himself?" Peter asked the twins.

"It couldn't have been," Emil answered. "Because Uncle John limps."

But Erna, turning quickly as the great door of the

castle swung open, exclaimed, "Let's ask him. Here he comes!"

In another minute both twins were rushing toward an old gentleman who limped into the entrance hall with a faintly bewildered expression on his face. Peter introduced himself and Judy. When John Dent had found a seat on one of the stone benches in the almost empty room, he sighed and began to explain where he had been.

"I had things to do—lots of things. I had to get to town, so I hitched a ride with some stranger. My old housekeeper lives there. She quarreled with Boggs and left us before I hurt my leg. Afterwards I was at his mercy. He figures I still can't move from my bed." He chuckled as he explained how he had fooled the caretaker by hiding in the suit of armor which supported his leg so that he walked without a limp. "Where is he?" he asked. "I sent the police to throw him out."

"Everybody sent the police," Peter laughed. "You didn't identify yourself, did you, Mr. Dent?"

"Why should I?" he asked. "I didn't know I was missing until I read it in the paper. Nobody's bothered with me for two years. How did I know a little trip into town was going to cause all this commotion? I spent the night with some relatives I looked up, grand-children of Debby's."

"Named Twinkle?" asked Judy.

"No, Meinkle. How'd you guess so close?"

"Granny told us how she and Debby used to have gay parties here before Debby left to marry Mr. Twinkle as they called him then. She said you'd promised her a party."

"Sure I did. Thought I'd surprise her, though, with a real big one. I've been inviting people, among other things. There's quite a tribe of Debby's descendants living here and in New York. I asked the whole lot of them." He turned to the twins. "I told you not to worry about Granny's birthday, that Uncle John would fix up the castle. Boggs carted off my furniture, but I figured we could rent some chairs from the funeral parlor and maybe use paper dishes. There's not a plate nor a piece of silver left."

"That won't be necessary," observed Peter. "Here comes the moving van with your furniture now."

Quickly he told John Dent how and where it had been found. Judy ran ahead of the moving van to reassure Granny, but stopped at the foot of the stairs.

"The suit of armor!" she exclaimed. "It's back in place."

John Dent seemed as surprised as she was to find it there. "Now I wonder how that happened," he said. "I left it in the woods after I let the children out. Must have walked here by itself."

"That is strange," agreed Judy. "You say you let the twins out of the dungeon, but didn't you let us out, too? Someone unlocked the door a little after midnight."

He shook his head.

"How could I?" he asked. "I was in town by that time."

The mystery remained unsolved until the following afternoon when Granny's party was in full swing.

The party was all Judy had hoped for—and more. One hundred guests were there, among them many of Judy's friends. They had all been rounded up, from the youngest to the oldest. It pleased Granny that there were exactly a hundred. And how very pleased she was to find that a hundred candles illuminated the great dining hall! Around them, cut in squares for easy serving, was the largest birthday cake Judy had ever seen. Lois and Lorraine had supervised the baking of it, which had been done in sections. There were a hundred presents, too. Everybody had brought something.

"Some I'll just have to save. There's too much for an old lady," sighed Granny. "But maybe you'll let me share what I can't use."

"Of course, Granny. Do anything you like with them."

Everybody called her Granny, even her neighbors. They were all her friends now.

"We really were all the time," one neighbor confided. "We let that caretaker fill our heads full of superstitious nonsense, and if any mistakes were made, you can blame him."

"And me," Horace confessed, "for reporting rumors instead of facts, but I'll make up for it when I report this party."

"I made a few mistakes myself," Granny admitted, "but I'm not too old to learn. You with the black cat!"

Judy had never been addressed quite like that before. She didn't have Blackberry with her, but she knew whom Granny meant.

"Yes?" she asked eagerly.

"Bring him to see me some time. I like cats."

"I'll lend you Blackberry any time you say," replied Judy. "He feels at home in the castle already."

Granny was told how Blackberry had found the dungeon.

"Mr. Boggs shut us in down there on purpose," Judy ended the story, "but there was another door he didn't know would open, and someone rescued us. Are you sure it wasn't you, Mr. Dent? He was wearing the suit of armor."

Soon everyone was questioning John Dent about the armor. He readily admitted that he had hidden inside it to spy on Boggs. He even admitted having been by the wall at the time Judy and her friends first saw their "man from Mars."

"I had just finished opening the wall into the dungeon," he explained. "Maybe that was why you thought I went through it. I couldn't climb down the ladder with my bad leg so I had to uncover the old door. It took me all afternoon working in all that rain and hail, but I got the twins out and saved the birthday present they had for Granny."

He got no further. The twins' cry of "Open it! Open it!" drowned out all other voices.

Their small fingers helped Granny's old ones undo the ribbon and blue paper in which John Dent had wrapped what proved to be a fairly large strongbox.

"I remember this. It was my father's—" Granny began.

But again came excited cries of "Open it! Open it!"

Finally, the strongbox was opened. Everyone crowded around gasping at the sight of the stacks of bills and gold pieces.

When Granny realized the purchase money had been found, she could only murmur, "Thank the Lord! Thank the Lord!" And finally, her eyes filling with tears, "Thank the Lord that he let me live to see my man's name cleared of shame. Emil, little Emil, you should be proud—"

"We are proud, Granny," father and son said together.

Hearing them, Erna announced, "I'm proud, too." And Judy kissed her to show her that she should be.

"There were so many conflicting stories it's no wonder we were confused," Judy said, "but here's what must really have happened. Emil Joerg, Granny's late husband, really did refund the purchase money to her father. But I suppose he didn't want to carry all that money around with him—"

"Or maybe he was afraid it would be stolen," put in Honey, helping Judy piece the story together.

"Perhaps. Anyway, we know he did hide it behind the stone and probably carved the arrow there, meaning to return for it or reveal the hiding place to his daughter."

"That was Granny, wasn't it?" the twins asked.

"Yes, it was Granny. Her father built the castle, but now the door to the dungeon was closed and it was a long way around to the front gate. He must have tried to climb over the wall the way you twins did—"

"And fell? We fell, too," Erna said. "Was Grandpa Olsen dead when they found him?"

"Yes, and the money was gone. But now we know what happened to it, don't we? And after all these years Granny has it to do whatever she likes with—"

"But why is she thanking the Lord for it when *we* found it?" Emil asked.

"I think," Judy replied, "that Granny is thanking the Lord for the wonderful long life she's had. Don't you?"

Soon Granny remembered to thank the twins and everyone else who had helped her celebrate her birthday. Never had the castle resounded to such merriment as followed. There was violin music for dancing by the castle ghost himself.

"I guess there's some of the little boy left in me yet," chuckled John Dent. "I did enjoy scaring Boggs with this fiddle. I didn't know he had any part in the thieving that's been going on along the turnpike, but I suspected he was up to something—which reminds me, we have someone else to thank."

"Granny did thank the Lord," Erna began.

"I know, but what about the knight who rescued these two young ladies from the dungeon?"

Now that the music had stopped, everybody's attention turned to the suit of armor that stood in its old place at the foot of the stairs. Lois and Lorraine gazed at the figure wonderingly. So did Honey. To them it was still their man from Mars.

Granny's old eyes twinkled in amusement, and all her friends stopped reminiscing long enough to watch, as John Dent walked over and made a deep bow before the figure of armor.

"It's good to see you back, old fellow," he said, shaking the mailed hand. "Maybe you can tell us how you got here."

The twins screamed with laughter.

"Uncle John is pretending the armor can talk when he isn't in it!"

"Someone besides Uncle John might be inside,"

Mrs. Joerg said a little fearfully to her husband. "If a thief—"

But Peter reassured her that he was keeping close watch on Granny's present.

Horace tapped on the breastplate.

"Anybody home?" he asked politely.

The girls backed away, giggling, all but Judy. She raised the visor to find nothing but emptiness.

"My knight!" wailed Honey in mock alarm. "He's vanished. I'll never be able to thank him for rescuing me."

"Do you really want to?" asked Horace.

"Of course, Horace. But I know it wasn't Mr. Dent. He spent the night in town, and who else—"

"I'll bet I know who else," Judy interrupted as her brother began to grin. "All right, smarty!" she said. "Maybe we were silly to let a man dressed up in armor scare us, but if you were the man—"

"You, Horace?"

He admitted it rather sheepishly.

"You see, I found the hardware in the woods where John Dent left it. That stuff is heavy, so I slipped inside. Easiest way to carry it, you know. Then I heard you girls calling from behind that door in the wall, and it happened that the key was right in the lock—"

"Oh, Horace! What a break for us!" Judy exclaimed.

"It certainly was. Anyway I used it to rescue two

fair damsels in distress. Unfortunately Peter and the police had the same idea. My position would have been a little hard to explain, so I hurried around to the castle and placed the old fellow back where he seemed to belong. Then I raced off to the paper with my story, which wasn't such a wild guess after all."

"I see," Judy said. "So there were two knights."

"But only one suit of armor," Peter put in. "Times are tough all over," he laughed. "Now what, Angel?" he asked, when Judy remained thoughtful. "Are you wondering when another mystery will turn up for us to solve?"

"I am wondering," Judy admitted, "not about another mystery, but about that birthday cake with a hundred candles on it. Granny's ready to pass it around! If we don't hurry there won't be a piece left for us. Yes, Granny, we're coming! We wouldn't miss this for anything in the world."

And *you* won't want to miss Judy's next exciting adventure—THE TRAIL OF THE GREEN DOLL. When Judy and Peter follow it, all sorts of strange things begin to happen—trees talk, a magician is tricked by his own magic—and at the end of the trail lies the biggest surprise of all. Be sure to read it!

Printed in the United States
119492LV00002B/97-156/P

9 781429 090469